Phonetics for Speech Pathology

Phonetics for Speech Pathology

Martin J. Ball

Taylor & Francis
London • New York • Philadelphia

| UK | Taylor & Francis Ltd, 4 John St, London WC1N 2ET |
| USA | Taylor & Francis Inc., 1900 Frost Road, Suite 101, Bristol, PA 19007 |

British Library Cataloguing in Publication Data

Ball, Martin J.
    Phonetics for speech pathology
    1. Phonetics
    I. Title
    414
    ISBN 0-85066-467-5

Library of Congress Cataloging-in-Publication Data available on request

Typeset by Chapterhouse, The Cloisters, Formby

Printed in Great Britain by Taylor & Francis (Printers) Ltd, Basingstoke

Contents

Part III Auditory Phonetics

Appendices: Phonetic Symbols and Notes on Transcription

List of Figures and Tables

Figures

Tables

Acknowledgements

I am grateful to publishers and authors for permission to reproduce their figures as listed below:

Figures 8.1, 8.2, 8.3, 8.4, 8.5, 8.6, 9.1, 9.2, 9.3, Edinburgh University Press (D. Abercrombie, *Elements of General Phonetics*); Figures 1.1, 3.2, 5.1, 5.2, 5.3, 5.4, 6.1, 6.2, Edinburgh University Press (J.C. Catford, *Fundamental Problems in Phonetics*).

Figures 23.1, 23.2, 23.3, 23.4, 23.5, 24.1, College Hill Press (W.H. Perkins and R.D. Kent, *Textbook of Functional Anatomy of Speech, Language and Hearing*).

Figures 1.2, 3.1, Donald Dew and Paul J. Jensen, (*Phonetic Processing, The Dynamics of Speech, Charles E. Merrill*).

Figure 17.4, Kay Elemetrics Corp.

Figure 26.1a, Gallaudet University Press.

Figure 26.1b, Royal National Institute for the Deaf.

Figure 26.2, Paget Gorman Society.

Figure 26.3, National Centre for Cued Speech.

Figure 27.2, Methuen (J.G. Wolff, *Language, Brain and Hearing*).

Figure 31.1, E. Legin and Chris Code.

Figure 32.1, Daniel S. Beasley

I am also grateful to the following colleagues for help in producing the figures listed below:

Figure 12.1, Chris Code.

Figure 12.2, Fiona Gibbon.

Figures 17.1, 17.3, 17.4, 18.1, 19.1, 19.2, 19.3, 20.1, 20.2, 20.3, 20.4, 21.1, 21.2, 22.2, 22.3, Robert H. McClurkin at Kay Elemetrics Corp.

Figures 17.2, 18.3, 18.4, 19.4, 20.5, Nigel Hewlett.

Preface

This book is designed to be an introductory text in phonetics for students following courses in speech pathology and therapy. To this end, the various topics, where appropriate, include information on normal and disordered speech. However, it is worth stressing that the book is not intended to be a guide to speech pathology, but to complement courses that will explore more fully those areas of communicative disorders touched upon while discussing phonetics.

The book is divided into three roughly equal parts covering the main approaches to phonetic study: articulatory, acoustic and the much neglected auditory phonetics. It is particularly important to include phonetic aspects of hearing and perception for speech pathology students, many of whom will be involved to some extent with audiological measurement. However, again I must introduce a *caveat:* this book will not train students to undertake audiometric techniques, any more than it will train them to use the other articulatory or acoustic procedures discussed in the first two parts of the book.

The chapters in Part I and Part II generally conclude with a short section linking the theoretical aspects of the chapter to speech problems of various types. In Part III the procedure is somewhat different. The first three chapters cover various aspects of hearing, followed by a complete chapter on hearing impairment, and another on audiological measurement. This part concludes with a series of chapters describing various perceptual techniques that have been used for both research and remediation in speech pathology.

Each chapter in the book ends with a further reading section. Normally this is not intended to be an in depth list, as the recommended reading must still be suitable for the audience, i.e. undergraduate students. The intention is to direct the student towards other introductory or straightforward books which may add a different dimension to the discussion, particularly in the area of disordered speech. Occasionally, however, more advanced texts and academic articles are referenced if this will add to the understanding of the topic.

As noted above, the book is aimed at first-year students, and the tripartite structure may well recommend it to courses structured around a three-term academic year. However, a two-semester arrangement can also be easily accommodated, as the first sixteen chapters can be easily followed by a break before undertaking the last sixteen. Indeed, the parts can be taken in any order, though chapters in Parts II and III do assume a knowledge of the phonetic symbols introduced in Part I.

Throughout the book the correct use of phonetic symbolization and the importance of adequate transcription in the clinic is stressed. To this end, the main symbols of the IPA are introduced, together with symbols for disordered speech (mostly those of the PRDS group). While these are explained and illustrated in the text, I have also included an appendix which lists the symbols and gives notes on transcription.

Also important for clinical phonetics is the use of instrumental transcription. Here, however, we face somewhat of a problem, as different training establishments have different amounts of access to such instrumentation. I have taken the opportunity to illustrate certain less usual techniques (such as aerometry and palatography), but have concentrated the discussion on a technique that many courses will be able to use: spectrography. I make no apology for the concentration on spectrography in Part II, as it remains the major tool in the investigation of acoustic phonetics. Therefore, the information in these chapters will serve as a background to the students' own work in this area, and an invaluable source of information to those who do not have the opportunity to use this equipment.

Finally, I would like to thank those who helped in the preparation of this text, and in particular Kay Elemetrics and Nigel Hewlett for their aid in preparing many of the figures. My thanks must go mostly though to Nicole whose help let me get most of this book written on my trips to Bonn, and to Chris Code for his careful reading of the text and many helpful suggestions for improvements. All remaining shortcomings are my responsibility.

PART I
Articulatory Phonetics

CHAPTER 1

The vocal organs

Phonetics is the study of human speech, and the first stage of the production of a speech signal is the organic phase: the utilization of the vocal organs. What exactly constitute the vocal organs is difficult to define, as they were not primarily designed for speech at all, but have had their primary functions adapted. In its widest possible sense the term should include the brain, where speech is planned, and neuromuscular activity where the plans are executed. For our purposes, however, we will concentrate on the *vocal tract*, here defined as the entire respiratory tract from the lungs to the nasal cavity together with the oral cavity (Figure 1.1).

The functions of the vocal tract in terms of speech production are numerous. Firstly, a stream of air must be set into motion for any sound wave to be created. This is termed *initiation*, and is discussed in Chapter 2. Then it is usually the case that the air-stream is given an overall 'shape' by passing through the larynx in a process termed *phonation* (see Chapter 3). The stream of air needs to have a series of individual sounds made on it through *articulation* (see Chapters 5–10). Finally, we must note that broader features of the speech signal (such as pitch and intensity, and groupings of speech sounds) have to be managed (see Chapters 4 and 11).

For us to understand how these aspects take place, we must have some knowledge of the important organs within the vocal tract; to do this we will look at the *lungs*, the *trachea*, the *larynx*, the *pharynx*, the *oral cavity*, and the *nasal cavity*.

Lungs

We can characterize the lungs as a pair of bellows, drawing in and expelling air, primarily for breathing purposes, though adaptable for speech production.

The lungs are in fact a pair of organs of an elastic, spongy nature. They consist of many small air sacs (*alveoli*) which open into larger tubes called *bronchioles* ending in the two *bronchi* which come together at the base of the trachea (Figure 1.1). The lungs are contained within the *pleura*: an air-tight chamber within the thoracic cavity, and are bounded by the rib-cage, and underneath by the diaphragm.

Figure 1.1 Vocal organs

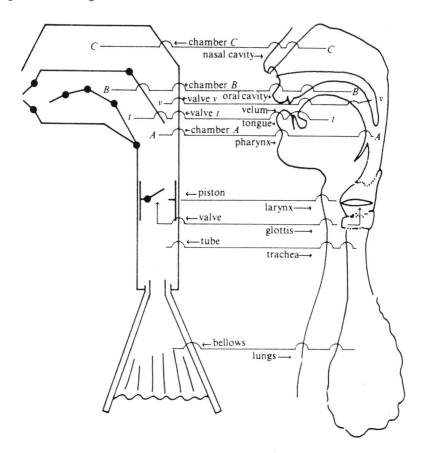

Inflation and deflation of the lungs is partly effected by muscular activity, and partly by gravity. The thoracic cavity is expanded by means of the external intercostal muscles of the rib-cage, thus creating a negative pressure in the pleura. To equalize pressure, air is drawn into the lungs, expanding them. The full lungs collapse under their own weight, and aided by the internal intercostal muscles, air is expelled from the lungs, though they never empty completely.

Trachea

This is also known as the 'windpipe' and is a semi-flexible tube consisting of rings of cartilage which are open at the back. It is approximately 11 cm long. When lung air is being used for speech, it is forced up the trachea to the larynx.

Larynx

The larynx is also made of cartilage (and includes tissue and muscle), and can be considered an extension to, or a part of, the trachea. The base of the larynx is called the *cricoid cartilage*, but this is also the top ring of the trachea, though unlike the others it is closed at the back (Figure 1.2). The *thyroid cartilage* is located above the cricoid cartilage and articulates with its side. It is open at the back, and has been described as looking like a snow-plough (the front part of this plough is what we see as the 'Adam's apple'). The *arytenoid cartilages* are the two small pyramid-like structures situated on top of the near part of the cricoid cartilage. From these two, forward to the interior of the front of the thyroid cartilage, run two parallel muscles: the *vocal folds* (or *vocal cords*, *vocal ligaments*).

Figure 1.2 Front and back views of the larynx

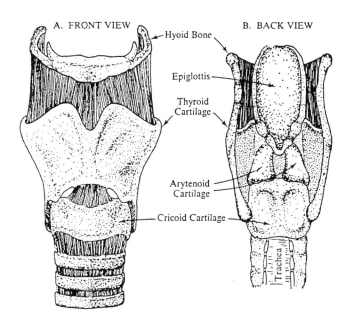

The space between the vocal folds is the *glottis*. This can change shape according to the activity of the vocal folds. The lateral position of the folds is controlled by movements of the arytenoid cartilages; their tension is controlled by the backwards–forwards movement of the thyroid cartilage. The folds themselves can assume various differences of shape, but are normally wedge-shaped. They play an important role in phonation (see Chapter 3).

Although the glottis can be open as well as closed, it always offers some resistance to an outward air flow (thus accelerating it), as the maximal glottis opening still covers just under half the cross-sectional area of the trachea. The larynx can be raised or lowered by several mm via the extrinsic laryngeal muscles.

Pharynx

The pharynx is the chamber immediately above the larynx reaching up to the rear of the nasal cavity. The lower part is sometimes termed the oropharynx, with the upper part as the nasopharynx.

The pharynx operates as a resonating chamber, to increase the volume of the air flow. It is possible to alter the volume of this chamber (and thus affect sound quality), although such alterations are not great. They are effected by raising the larynx via the extrinsic laryngeal muscles, by drawing the tongue and epiglottis back into the pharynx, or by contraction of the back wall of the pharynx.

Oral cavity and nasal cavity

The oral cavity, or mouth, plays an important role in articulation. It is another resonating chamber, but is able to be modified in numerous ways. Most important in this respect are the following: the tongue, the teeth, lips, alveolar ridge, hard palate, soft palate (velum), and uvula. The velum is moveable, and closes or opens entry from the oropharynx into the nasal cavity. When the nasal cavity is coupled into the oral cavity, an extra resonating chamber is available. However, the nasal cavity cannot be modified.

Disordered speech

As we will see in future chapters, much disordered speech is due to high level organizational problems, or neurological impairment. However, there are certain problems that are due to physical disability or fault. In terms of the vocal organs, the most common of these organic malfunctions is cleft palate or other forms of velopharyngeal inadequacy (i.e. the inability to control the opening and closing of the velum). Other disabilities such as tongue-tie can also occur, and some can result from surgery, for example laryngectomy and glossectomy (see Chapter 3 for observations or laryngectomy).

While speech is still usually possible with cleft palate, certain sound types are difficult to produce, and there is generally an all-pervasive hypernasality. With this type of patient, surgery is the only answer; but even following successful surgery patients often have difficulty changing disordered speech patterns. Cleft palate is returned to in Chapter 7.

Further reading

Most of the standard texts on phonetics have details on the organs of speech. Examples are Brosnahan and Malmberg (1970) chapter 3; Abercrombie (1967) chapter 2; Ladefoged (1975) chapter 1; and the two books of Catford: his major work (1977, chapter 2), and his recent text (1988, chapter 1). However, there is a major work on anatomy and physiology aimed at the phonetician, which contains probably the fullest description of the vocal organs (Perkins and Kent, 1986). Several chapters from part one of this book will be of help in giving further information to that contained in this chapter, notably chapters 2 and 3, and to a lesser extent 5 and 6.

CHAPTER 2

Initiation

To produce speech, a column of air must be set in motion somewhere within the vocal tract. Onto this air-stream modifications are made, such as phonation and articulation, to produce the various sounds of speech. To set air in motion requires movement of an organ or a group of organs in a way similar to a pair of bellows, or to a piston. The movements of these organs (the *initiators*) will result in pressure changes in the surrounding air; these pressure changes can be negative or positive depending upon whether the movement of the organs increases or decreases the volume of the adjacent vocal tract. Positive air pressure changes generally result in an outflow of air in order to equalize pressure, negative air pressure changes generally result in an inflow of air. The term air-stream mechanism is often used to describe this process. Pressure, and thereby direction, is one important parameter in the description of initiation. Positive pressure is termed compressive, and the resultant airflow is usually egressive. Negative pressure is termed rarefactive or suction, and the resultant air flow is usually ingressive.

The other main parameter in the classification of initiation is the location of the initiators. Although small air flows can be initiated in numerous locations, in linguistic terms we are only interested in three locations (see later for a description of oesophageal initiation): the lungs, the larynx, and the mouth. Initiation from the lungs is termed pulmonic, and in normal speech we only find an egressive pulmonic air-stream; initiation in the larynx is termed glottalic (or laryngeal/pharyngeal) and both ingressive and egressive air-streams can be found in normal speech (though not in English); initiation in the mouth is termed velaric (or oralic), and an ingressive air-stream can be found in normal speech (though only extralinguistically in English, see below). We will now examine these different air-streams in more detail.

Pulmonic initiation

For pulmonic egressive air-streams, the lungs decrease in volume which generates a positive pressure in the whole vocal tract (or if the glottis is closed, in the subglottal

8

vocal tract). The resultant air flow is comparatively great, with a maximum length in time of up to 25 sec, though normally only 2–10 sec of speech occurs on one exhalation. The intercostal (or rib-cage) muscles that are used to control the lungs in normal breathing, have a somewhat modified function in speech, in that the external intercostals act as a 'brake', slowing down the emptying of the lungs and thus giving us extra time for speech.

Pulmonic egressive air-streams are the most usual in speech, in that all known languages use them, and further, for languages that use other air-streams, pulmonic egressive sounds are still the great majority of the sounds used. This air-stream is particularly suitable for phonation (see Chapter 3), as the vocal folds are better adapted for air passing up through them from below than the other way round.

For a pulmonic ingressive air-stream, the initiator action of the lungs occurs during inhalation, as air rushes in to equalize the negative pressure that occurs with the increase of lung volume. As noted previously, the vocal folds are not well adapted to air being drawn through them from above, so speech on this air-stream has a rough quality to it. This air-stream is not regularly used in any known language, though it can occur as a feature of rapid counting, or as a way of disguising one's voice. If needed, sounds uttered on this air-stream can be phonetically transcribed with a special diacritic as follows:- [m̰, t̰, z̰, l̰] etc.

Glottalic initiation

To produce a glottalic egressive air-stream, the initiator — the larynx — is moved swiftly upwards by the extrinsic laryngeal muscles. The glottis is kept tightly closed to prevent air leakage, so the entire structure acts as a piston and creates a positive pressure change in the supraglottal vocal tract. However, the volume of air affected (which thus constitutes the air-stream on which speech is made) is small, as it is contained in the space between the glottis and whichever articulatory stricture is in place within the oral cavity. For this reason, we generally find glottalic egressive air-streams being used to produce single sounds only within a stretch of otherwise pulmonic egressive sounds.

Various types of sounds can be produced on this air-stream: stops, affricates and fricatives (see Chapter 5 for descriptions of these terms). The general name given to these sounds is ejective, although some authorities restrict this name to the stops produced on this air-stream. If need be, the terms ejective stops, ejective fricatives etc. can be employed. Other names used instead of ejectives are glottalized or checked (US usage), recursives (European usage) and abruptives (Soviet usage). In phonetic transcription the diacritic ['] is used to denote an ejective, e.g. [p', k', tʃ', f']. Ejectives are fairly common, occurring in Caucasian languages such as Georgian, some Indian languages including Gujerati, languages in the Far East, American Indian languages and many in Africa among others.

To create a glottalic ingressive air-stream, the reverse of the above takes place:

the larynx is pulled downwards creating a negative pressure in the supraglottal vocal tract, and air rushes in to equalize the pressure. The sounds thus produced are very rare linguistically, being reported from only one language (see Catford, 1977, p. 71). They can be termed 'reverse ejectives', and are transcribed as: [ɓ̇, k̇, ʧ̇', f̓] or [p', k̰', t̰ʃ', f̰'].

Much more common is a voiced glottalic ingressive air-stream. In reality this is a mixture of glottalic ingressive and pulmonic egressive. In this form of initiation the glottis is not kept tightly closed, so as the larynx is jerked downwards, lung air escapes through the glottis causing the vocal folds to vibrate. Thus we have ingressive air flowing in to equalize the negative pressure in the supraglottal tract combined with egressive lung air flowing out to equalize the positive pressure in the subglottal tract. Only stop sounds are known in natural languages with this air stream, and they are generally termed implosives. They are transcribed as [ɓ, ɗ, ɠ]. They are found in many languages including those of West Africa, and some Indian languages (including Sindhi) among others.

Velaric initiation

Velaric ingressive air-streams need a closure between the back of the tongue and the velum, together with an articulatory closure further forward in the oral cavity. This traps a small pocket of air between these two closures. If the centre of the tongue is then moved downwards and/or backwards, this pocket is increased in volume and a negative pressure created. On the release of the articulatory closure, air flows inwards to equalize this pressure imbalance. Only a small amount of air is involved with these sounds, so we tend to find them surrounded by pulmonic egressive sounds in speech. Various types of sound are potentially possible with this air stream, though only stop-like ones are found in normal speech, being termed *clicks*. They have their own phonetic symbols: [ʘ, ǀ, ǃ, ǂ].

Clicks are found mainly in languages in southern Africa (e.g. Bushman, Hottentot, Xhosa, Zulu), but are used extralinguistically (e.g. to express annoyance or encouragement) in many other languages. Combinations of clicks with oral and nasal pulmonic egressive sounds also occur, and can be transcribed as [k͡ǀ, g͡ǀ, ŋ͡ǀ] etc.

A velaric egressive air stream can be created in the same way as above, with the exception that the air pocket is reduced in volume by tongue movement rather than increased. 'Reverse clicks' are not known to occur in the normal speech of any known language. If necessary, they can be transcribed as [ʘ⃗, ǀ⃗, ǃ⃗, ǂ⃗].

Disordered speech

It is not uncommon to encounter patients presenting with abnormal use of air-streams. Inappropriate use of a pulmonic ingressive air flow can be heard, as can the substitution of glottalic ingressive (more rarely glottalic egressive) sounds for certain pulmonic egressive ones. For example, the realization of /kæt/ by [kæt'], or [k'æt'], or even [k't'] can occur.

Clicks and reverse clicks are rare with patients, and this usage would be characterized as a more extreme disturbance than those noted above. The most extreme effect has been termed 'zero air-stream'. This occurs when for either one or several sounds a patient makes appropriate (or at least some) articulatory gestures, but fails to produce an air-stream. The 'Phonetic Representation of Disordered Speech' group (PRDS) recommend these be transcribed as: [(f), (m)], etc.

The preceding can be found with just single speech sounds, or more pervasively may affect whole stretches of speech. We must now consider an air-stream mechanism which can be substituted entirely for the usual pulmonic egressive. In patients who have undergone laryngectomy, the usual pulmonic egressive air-stream may no longer be of use as phonation is no longer possible (but see Chapter 3 for discussion of artificial larynxes).

In these circumstances, some patients are trained to use oesophageal (or oesophagic) speech. This uses an air-stream released from the oesophagus. The air being forced passed the oesophageal sphincter produces vibrations that can take the part of phonatory activity. Although the amount of air is less than pulmonic egressive, it is generally enough to produce several speech sounds, and speakers used to this method can produce quite long stretches of speech on this air-stream.

Further reading

Initiation is covered by most phonetic texts, and discussion can be found in Ladefoged (1975) chapter 6; Brosnahan and Malmberg (1970) chapter 4.2; Abercrombie (1967) chapter 2; Catford (1977) chapters 3 and 5 (these go into the aerodynamics of speech production in some detail), and Catford (1988) chapter 2. Relevant chapters of Perkins and Kent (1986), especially chapter 3, outline the physiology of the initiation process.

CHAPTER 3

Phonation

A pulmonic egressive air flow, once created, has to pass through two further stages before it emerges as what we perceive as a string of speech sounds: *phonation* and *articulation*.

Phonation takes place in the larynx, or more particularly in the glottis (the space between the vocal folds). Phonatory activity is activity by the vocal folds which affects the sound quality of the air stream. The larynx is also used in speech as an initiator (see Chapter 2) and as a place of articulation (see Chapter 6), but here we are concerned only with the production of 'voice' types (as phonation is commonly known).

The two most important phonation types linguistically are 'voiced' and 'voiceless', as all known languages utilize these two, many of them using these two exclusively. However, there are other types, and as voice disorders present commonly in the speech pathology clinic, it is important that we give here a thorough account of phonation types.

Figure 3.1 is a representation of the larynx, with some of the important structures labelled. Later in the chapter these will be referred to in describing the various phonation types. In our description we will look first at type of phonatory stricture, then at location of phonatory stricture ('stricture' is the term used in phonetics to describe the bringing together of any two vocal organs).

Type of phonatory stricture

Phonatory stricture refers to the amount of vocal fold approximation there is during any particular phonation type. There are four main degrees of stricture: voiceless, whisper, voice and creak.

For a *voiceless* phonation the glottis is open (between 60 per cent and 95 per cent of the maximal opening). Two varieties of voiceless phonation can be recognized dependent on the volume–velocity of the air flow: low volume–velocity flow produces a smooth, laminar phonation termed *nil-phonation* (e.g. such

Figure 3.1 The intrinsic muscles of the larynx

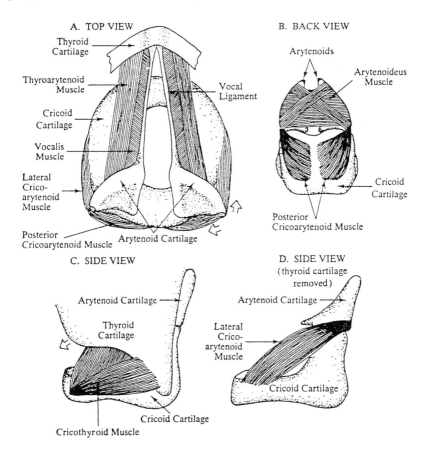

sounds as [f, s, ʃ], while high volume–velocity flow produces a turbulent phonation termed *breath* (as with [h]). The following English phonemes (i.e. contrastive sounds) are voiceless: /p, t, k, ʧ, f, θ, s, ʃ, h/.

With *whisper* the glottis is narrowed to less than 25 per cent of the maximal opening. The air flow is strongly turbulent and creates a rich, hushing type of sound. Normal phonation is often replaced by whisper when speakers wish to disguise their voices or reduce loudness. When this is done, vowels and voiced sounds are transferred to whisper, while voiceless sounds are unaffected.

For *voice* the glottis is closed, and the vocal folds are subjected to varying degrees of tension so that they vibrate, and emit periodic high velocity puffs of air. Higher voice registers (including falsetto) are produced in a similar way, although complete glottal closure may not be present. The following English phonemes are partially or completely voiced: /b, d, g, dʒ, m, n, ŋ, v, ð, z, ʒ, l, r, w, j/ and all the vowels and diphthongs.

Creak also requires a closed glottis, but the low subglottal pressure and low volume–velocity of the air flow results in low-frequency periodic puffs of air through a small gap near the anterior end of the vocal folds. Some English speakers with very low-pitched voices demonstrate creak, but it is also used linguistically in some languages.

There are also four possible combinations of these preceding phonation types: breathy voice; whispery voice; whispery creak and creaky voice.

Breathy voice has a glottis less open than for voicelessness, but more open than for whisper. The vocal folds are allowed to 'flap' in the high volume–velocity air flow. This phonation cannot be long maintained. *Whispery voice* (or 'murmur') involves the combination of relaxed yet vibrating vocal folds, with a turbulent air flow escaping through a chink to produce whisper. Unfortunately, some authorities call this phonation type 'breathy voice' which can lead to confusion with the previous type. *Whispery creak* is similar to murmur, except that there is lower frequency vibration of the vocal folds. *Creaky voice* is a combination of voiced and creaked phonation in a way which is not totally clear. Again, creaky voice can often be heard in slow, 'drawling' speakers of English.

The terms *fortis* and *lenis* ('strong' and 'weak', equivalent to the terms *tense* and *lax* for vowels, see Chapter 9) are often applied to consonants. It is generally reckoned that voiceless consonants are fortis in that they involve more muscular effort and a greater output of air than voiced, or lenis, ones. Although useful as a phonological label, there is still some debate as to the phonetic validity of this distinction (see Catford, 1977, pp. 199 f, and more recently, Kohler, 1984).

Location of phonatory stricture

Figure 3.2 shows a view of the glottis from above, and on it are marked the four possible locations of the stricture types noted above. These are: full glottal; anterior; posterior and ventricular.

Full glottal is the normal location for most phonation types. Here, the entire length of the glottis (both the anterior or ligamental section and the posterior or arytenoidal section) act as a single structure with no restriction at any location.

With *anterior location*, the arytenoid cartilages are held together and only the ligamental part of the glottis participates in the phonation. Anterior voice is usually termed 'tense voice' (or 'sharp/tight voice').

With *posterior location*, the ligamental part of the glottis is closed, with phonation occurring at the arytenoidal end. This is generally an unusual location for phonation, but whisper can be produced here.

Ventricular phonation is in many respects different from the other locations we have examined. This is because it does not involve the vocal folds, but rather the 'false vocal folds' or 'ventricular bands' (see Figure 3.1) situated above the vocal folds. These bands can be used instead of the vocal folds to produce ventricular whisper, ventricular voice and ventricular creak.

Figure 3.2 The glottis

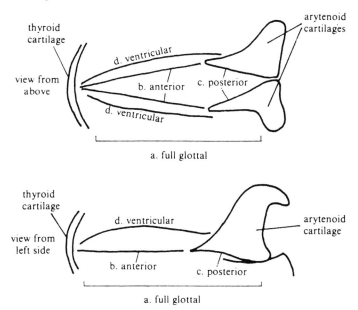

A combination of ventricular voice and glottal voice is possible, and is termed 'double-voice' or 'diplophonia'. It is particularly associated with certain types of jazz singing, but has also been recorded among the chanting of Tibetan monks (see Catford, 1977).

In this survey of normal phonation, we have not had the space to examine voice differences due to register (e.g. bass versus treble, etc.). These are discussed in detail in Catford (1977, p. 109f), and we return to the acoustic characteristics of voice resonance in Chapter 15.

Voice disorders

The term voice disorders encompasses more than disorders of phonation in traditional speech pathology terminology. Apart from phonation, the term can also refer to disorders of resonance (for example, hypernasality). These features are not discussed here, but some are referred to in other chapters.

In terms of disorders originating in the larynx, we mainly refer to a range of unusual or inappropriate voice qualities (or *timbres*), such as whisper, breathy voice, creak, etc. Structural interference to the air flow will produce a 'hoarse' quality which varies dependent upon what kind of obstruction is present, and where it is located. The common term for these phonation disorders is *dysphonia* (or where voice is totally absent: *aphonia*).

Dysphonia may be continual or intermittent, often depending upon the cause of the disorder. Cause may be divided into three main factors: developmental problems, organic disorders (such as the growth of vocal nodules, or cancerous growths), or psychological factors (which can be very common) and other functional problems (such as vocal fold abuse in singers, etc.). Full discussion of this complex area of speech pathology can be found in Greene (1973).

In Chapter 2 it was mentioned that one type of patient presenting in the speech pathology clinic was the laryngectomee. The removal of the larynx has implications for initiation, but also for phonation. Normal vocal fold activity is obviously lost in these patients, but nevertheless artificial phonatory activity is possible in an attempt to approximate to normal speech.

There are a range of 'artificial larynxes', including vibrators which are in reality 'buzz-producers', i.e. electronic devices capable of producing a high-frequency noise. This device is held against the throat, to produce the equivalent of voiced phonation. While this obviously sounds artificial, it at least gives these patients a way back to vocal communication.

Transcription of phonation

There is no clear agreement on how to transcribe the various phonation types we have investigated, though IPA diacritics do exist for some of them.

1. Voiceless. Unless otherwise shown by the symbol itself, voiceless phonation is shown by [o]. If applied to a 'voiced' symbol, it is usually interpreted as 'devoiced to some extent'. [od]~[do] imply 'initially devoiced' and 'finally devoiced' respectively. If 'breath' rather than nil-phonation needs to be shown, then [h] can be used: [hp]~[ph] mean pre- and postaspirated stops (see Chapter 8).
2. Whisper. No accepted diacritic exists, but the following is suggested: [̬].
3. Voice. Unless otherwise shown by the symbol itself, voiced phonation is shown by [̩]. Voicing that starts earlier, or continues longer than usual can be shown thus: [̞z]~[z ̞]. Partially voiced sounds that are normally voiceless can be shown as: [̞s]~[s ̞].
4. Creak. No accepted diacritic exists, but the following is suggested by Dalton and Hardcastle (1977): [~]. The suggestion of [̰] by Laver (1980) and Shriberg and Kent (1982) is rejected, as it has also been used for partially nasalized (see Chapter 7) and for pharyngealization (see Chapter 10).

The only combinatory type with an accepted diacritic is breathy voice (IPA, 1979), though Shriberg and Kent use this for what they call murmur: [̤].

To avoid problems from this type of confusion of terminology, it is suggested here that where no suitable diacritic exists, the combinatory types of phonatory stricture be transcribed using two diacritics from the list above, as follows:

5. breathy voice: [₀] or [..]
6. whispery voice: [:] or [··]
7. whispery creak: [⌢]
8. creaky voice: [⌣]

Location types also have no usual diacritics to distinguish them. In practice, anterior and ventricular are the only ones that need distinguishing from full glottal which last can remain unmarked. It is suggested here that superscript diacritics be used for location as follows (posterior included for completeness):

a. anterior: [ᴵᴼ]
b. posterior: [ᴼᴵ]
c. ventricular: [ᴴ]

Diplophonia (double voice) would be shown by [ᴴ], whereas [ᴴ] would stand for ventricular voice alone.

Symbolization may also be needed to show the varying types of hoarse voice quality that can be encountered in pathological speech. Describing different varieties of hoarseness is, however, a difficult and inexact science. It is suggested that, where necessary, a superscript capital-H be used to denote the onset of any degree of hoarseness: [ᴴ], with [⁻ᴴ] showing where this feature ends. For full details of usage of these symbols see Ball (1988b).

If the various voice qualities to be described are in fact continuous over stretches of speech, rather than occurring with single segments, it might be felt easier to avoid these diacritics, and resort instead to labelled bracketing of the relevant passages, or the use of the diacritic in + / − mode as with the hoarseness sign discussed earlier.

Further reading

Chapters 4 and 5 of Perkins and Kent (1986) discuss the physiology and anatomy of the various structures that contribute to phonatory activity. Phonation is discussed in particular detail in Catford (1977) in chapter 6. Catford's analysis is discussed in terms of possible symbolization by Ball (1988b), and earlier by Sprigg (1978).

Most other phonetic texts (as referred to in previous chapters) describe phonation, but there are also specialist texts on voice and phonation, the most important of which is probably Laver (1980). In terms of voice disorders, the classic text are Greene (1973) and Luchsinger and Arnold (1965), with more recent work by Aronsen (1980), Edels (1983), Stemple (1984) and Fawcus (1986).

CHAPTER 4

Syllables

We have seen how the vocal organs can initiate an air flow which in turn can be modified by other of the vocal organs to produce speech. Before we consider how individual speech sounds are 'shaped' from this air flow, we have to examine how the speech signal is organized into syllables.

Syllables have always played an important role in our perception of speech, and indeed, many early and current writing systems are based on the syllable as the minimal orthographic unit, rather than the sound segment. Most speakers of a language are able to identify the number of syllables any word has, but in English, for example, we are not always able to say precisely where syllable boundaries occur for certain words. Further, although we can identify the number of syllables a word has, we are not usually able to say how we reached our answer, or to produce an adequate description of what a syllable is.

It appears that we may indeed not all have precisely the same idea as to what a syllable is, or that we perceive them in slightly different ways. For example, in English there are some groups of words about which speakers disagree concerning numbers of syllables. These include '-ism' words (e.g. *catholicism, republicanism*): is the '-ism' ending one syllable or two? Other examples include -/il/ endings: *real, wheel*; centring diphthongs (in non-rhotic accents): *fire, wire, hour*; and examples with neighbouring vowels: *mediate, heavier*. So any theory of the syllable must be able to account for why we agree on most syllable counts, but disagree on these. Phoneticians have yet to agree on a comprehensive theory that adequately accounts for the syllable. The approaches made so far take either an acoustic or a physiological–articulatory stance.

Acoustic theories

The first of these is known as *sonority theory*. The sonority of a sound is its loudness relative to other sounds with the same length, stress and pitch. These values are relatively easy to work out instrumentally (see Chapter 14), and although not

Figure 4.1 The relative sonority values of some English sounds

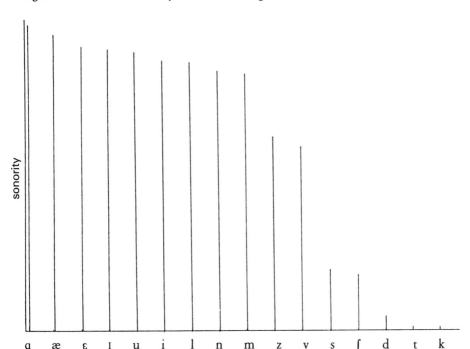

identical for all speakers, average values can be seen in Figure 4.1. We can see that low vowels have a greater sonority than high vowels, nasals have greater sonority than voiced fricatives, and that voiced stops and voiceless sounds all have very little sonority.

Sonority was used to define the syllable in the following way: by working out the sonority levels of each sound in a word it would be clear that a number of peaks of sonority existed in that word. These peaks of sonority coincide with the peaks of syllabicity, so that the number of peaks equals the number of syllables (see examples in Figure 4.2). This theory could explain why most people agree on the number of syllables most words have, but also why they disagree on '-ism' words, and the other examples given above. It may be that for some speakers the final [m] of '-ism' has a greater sonority than the preceding [z] (thus giving two peaks of sonority), whereas for others the opposite may be the case (thereby leaving only one peak).

Unfortunately, there are several examples where sonority theory falls down by failing to account for syllabicity. One of these involves initial /s/ + stop clusters in English. According to the theory, the word 'spa' has two peaks of sonority ([s] and [ɑ] have greater sonority than [p], as shown in Figure 4.2), but all of us would agree that it is a single syllable word.

Figure 4.2 Sonority values of the sounds in the word 'plant'

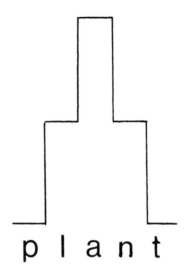

Another problem concerns syllabic consonants. Although the syllabic peak (the central part of the syllable) is generally a vowel, some languages allow certain consonants to take this role (one reason why we cannot count syllables by just counting vowels). For example, in English [l] and [n] and sometimes [m] can be syllabic peaks. Unfortunately, sonority theory seems unable to distinguish non-syllabic [l] and [n] from syllabic [l̩] and [n̩]. We can see this in alternative pronunciations that are available for words like 'meddling' (['med.l̩.ɪŋ]~ ['med.lɪŋ]) and 'brightening' (['braɪt.n̩.ɪŋ]~['braɪt.nɪŋ]), all of which will provide us with only two peaks of sonority.

In an attempt to get round these problems, a modification to the theory was suggested: *prominence theory*. According to this approach, syllables are marked by peaks of prominence, and prominence is defined in the following way: the relative prominence of two sounds depends partly on what their relative sonority would have been if they had had the same length, stress and pitch, but it also depends in part on their actual length, stress and pitch.

So it was argued that while the sonority of syllabic and non-syllabic consonants was the same, the prominence of syllabic consonants was greater, thus producing the extra peaks needed to mark the syllable. Unfortunately, to date, no satisfactory way of calculating prominence values has been devised, so we have to consider this version of the theory as at best unproved.

Physiological approach

The work of Stetson (1951), and later by phoneticians such as Ladefoged (1967) and

Catford (1977) has taken a different approach. This is to view syllabicity not as a property of the acoustic signal, but as a physiologically definable activity of the speaker.

Stetson suggested that every syllable is initiated by a 'chest-pulse', that is to say a measurable contraction of the rib cage muscles that help push out the pulmonic egressive air flow from the lungs. Ladefoged (1967), however, pointed out that there was not always a one-to-one relationship between chest-pulse, and for a time this theory was therefore not well regarded. However, work by Catford (1977) has shown that for English at least, syllables (and divisions of syllables, called 'feet') do in fact correspond to the power peaks of muscle activity.

In the long run, we will probably find that a combination of physiological, acoustic and indeed psychological definitions will be needed to fully comprehend the nature of the syllable. We will look next at how syllables are organized.

Structure of the syllable

Although syllabic structure is mainly of phonological concern, it is possible for us here to take a brief look at the phonetic framework that underlies this area. The classification of syllabic structure is often called 'phonotactics', and involves looking at what types of sound can occur where in a syllable. Before we can consider this point, however, we need to define what places of structure exist in a syllable.

The central part of syllable structure is the 'syllabic peak', usually represented by the abbreviation 'V' (not necessarily a vowel; see the discussion above on syllabic consonants). Apart from this central phase, there are two marginal phases: first the releasing phase (preceding V), and secondly the arresting phase (following V). These are both represented by the abbreviation 'C'. Although a syllable must have a V phase, in most languages the C phases are optional.

Let us take an example. In English we can have syllables containing just V, C + V, V + C and C + V + C:

C	V	C
	a	
m	ay	
	ai	d
m	ai	d

This arrangement can be shown as (C)V(C). If a language allows clusters of sound at the releasing or arresting phases (as English does) this can be shown as, for example, (C)(C)(C)V(C)(C)(C)(C), or more simply $C_{0-3}VC_{0-4}$. These patterns are very complicated, and some languages allow only basic, simple patterns, as Japanese: $C_{0-1}V\emptyset$; Chinese: $C_{0-1}VC_{0-1}$.

In polysyllabic words, rules of structure may change, and will of course need to be stated. Further, we have to be aware that syllable boundaries may occur at different places in similar words (this for example can occur in English but not in

French, though in English it is not always easy to agree on where boundaries occur in certain word types). As an example we can consider the following:

beekeeper	CV.CV –
beefeater	CVC.V –
teatray	CV.CCV
heatray	CVC.CV

Disordered speech

In disordered speech syllables can be affected in two ways: through deletion and/or through simplification. In normal phonological development there can be a process whereby weak syllables of polysyllabic words are deleted. This will not always lead to monosyllables, as a reduplicating process is also strong in early phonological development (giving us forms like 'mama', etc.). If this feature is retained it will be classified as disordered speech. Syllable deletion is usually attributable to the effects of stress and rhythm, and is discussed further in Chapter 11. However, some acquired speech disorders, apraxia of speech and some forms of aphasia, may result in drastic simplification of word and syllable structure.

Syllabic simplification refers to the loss of sounds at releasing and arresting phases. It is again very common in normal development to see a loss of all C segments at the arresting phase (syllable-final consonant deletion), and an overall simplification of clusters of consonants (cluster reduction). These processes can all be retained to become examples of delayed phonological development.

Further reading

Syllables tend to be neglected in many accounts of phonetics, though Abercrombie (1967) chapter 3 does discuss the problems of definition in some detail. Brosnahan and Malmberg (1970) also devote some space to the topic (in section 7.9). The second of these books also describes units between the syllable and the word, normally called 'the foot', and this topic is described in Abercrombie (1965) chapter 4. Ladefoged (1975) devotes the first part of his chapter 10 to syllable theory, but unlike most of the other references cited above, does not discuss types of syllable. Catford (1977, 1988) discusses syllable types and units like 'feet', but does not go into the controversy of defining the syllable (pp. 88f and pp. 178f respectively).

Most books on phonological disorders discuss the phenomenon of syllable deletion and simplification. Perhaps one of the best accounts is Grunwell (1987), in particular chapter 7.

CHAPTER 5

Manner of Articulation

We have examined so far how speech is produced and organized, but not yet in terms of individual speech sounds. In this and the following chapter we will be looking at the traditional classification of speech sounds in respect of the way in which they are articulated ('manner'), and the position of the articulators ('place'). In phonetics, articulation refers to the process of producing individual speech sounds, and the articulators are those vocal organs involved in this (e.g. tongue, lips, hard palate, velum, etc.).

Articulation requires the bringing together ('approximation') of two articulators to a greater or lesser degree to interfere with the air flow (see Chapter 2). The precise amount of interference depends on how close the articulators are brought to each other, and it is this that determines the manner of articulation.

Normal speech

In this section we will look at what manners of articulation are used in normal speech; not of any one language in particular, but of language in general.

When classifying articulation, phoneticians generally consider two dimensions within the oral cavity: the vertical dimension, and the lateral one (the horizontal one is that of place of articulation discussed in the next chapter). The lateral dimension refers to the fact that many types of sound can be pronounced with air flow either centrally over the tongue (median sounds), or laterally over one or both sides of the tongue (lateral sounds). Because most speech sounds found in natural language are median sounds, it is generally the case that this dimension is only mentioned in describing speech sounds if the sound is lateral, otherwise it is assumed to be median. We will return later to look at which manners of articulation are found laterally as well as centrally.

In describing the vertical dimension we will be considering pulmonic egressive sounds only, though we will look again at other air stream mechanisms later. The interference with the air stream in this dimension is often referred to as the 'degree

Figure 5.1 Degrees of stricture

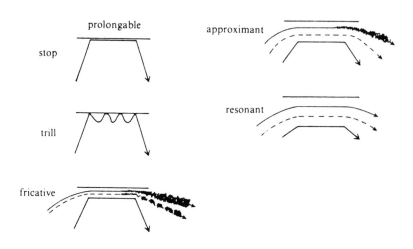

of stricture' (see Figure 5.1). The closest, or most extreme degree of stricture, is one where the articulators are brought into contact with each other. This contact is so firm that the flow of air is actually stopped behind this obstruction, and for this reason this manner of articulation is termed the 'stop'.

Stops are formed by bringing together two articulators, followed by a stage when the air stream is blocked off (this may last from 50 to 60 msec): the closure stage. This closure causes a build up of air pressure behind the stricture, and on release of the closure the air 'pops' out. These orally released stops are often termed *plosives*. The sounds [p, t, k, b, d, g] in English are usually pronounced as plosives. Stops may be made with the velum lowered, so that air pressure is not built up but escapes through the nasal cavity. These are termed 'nasal stops', e.g. [m, n, ŋ] in English, or often simply 'nasals', and are described further in Chapter 7. Further details of modifications to stop articulation are given in Chapter 8.

The next closest degree of stricture is termed *fricative*. As the name suggests, these sounds are heard as containing friction (or 'frication'). This comes about because the articulators are brought so close together that only a small, or narrow, channel is left for the air to escape. The laws of aerodynamics predict that an air stream (or any gas; see Chapter 2) that is forced down a narrow channel becomes turbulent. We perceive this turbulence as friction.

Apart from their place of articulation (Chapter 6) and phonation differences (Chapter 3), the main division of fricatives is dependent on the shape of the channel. One important distinction in this respect is that between grooved and slit fricatives (see Figure 5.2). An example from English can illustrate this: English [s] as in 'sink' is a grooved fricative — the channel down which the air escapes is a narrow central groove formed by the tongue. On the other hand, English [θ] as in 'think' is a slit fricative, in that the lower articulator (the tongue) is flattened, and the channel is fairly wide and flat. This distinction obviously cannot be applied to fricatives formed by the lips or at the back of the tongue, so a distinction based on the auditory features of fricatives is often found. The terms 'sibilant' and 'non-sibilant' are also used for grooved and slit fricatives respectively, but can also be extended to cover others of the class. The sounds [s, z, ʃ, ʒ] are termed sibilant, and have more acoustic energy and have a higher pitch than [f, v, θ, ð]. The more recent, phonological, distinction between 'strident' and 'non-strident' (i.e. greater or lesser acoustic 'noisiness') fricatives is felt by many phoneticians not to be as useful a distinction as that of sibilancy. According to this last view, [θ, ð,] are non-strident, while [f, v, s, z, ʃ, ʒ] are strident.

Figure 5.2 Channel shapes

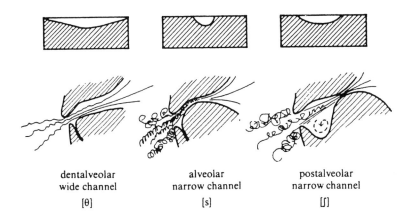

dentalveolar	alveolar	postalveolar
wide channel	narrow channel	narrow channel
[θ]	[s]	[ʃ]

The next degree of stricture is termed *approximant*. The air channel here is comparatively wide, and at least with voiced approximants, the air flow is not turbulent. Many approximants are articulatorily (and indeed perceptually) simply weaker (i.e. wider) versions of fricatives. An example of an English approximant is [ɹ] which is the usual pronunciation of 'r' in most accents.

One particular type of approximant (though classified separately by some phoneticians, e.g. Catford, 1977) is the *semi-vowel*. As the name suggests these are linked in articulation terms to vowels (mostly close vowels, see Chapter 9), but are not continuous (or prolongable) sounds like other approximants. Instead, these sounds are 'momentary', in that the articulators move away instantly after the semi-vowel is pronounced to take up position for the next sound. The English sounds [j] and [w] in 'yacht' and 'what' respectively would be classed as semi-vowels.

The fourth stricture type is the *resonant*, which is usually considered to equate with the category of 'vowel' (though strictly speaking there are certain differences). This type is not discussed here, but is examined fully in Chapter 9.

Technically speaking, all four of these stricture types are capable of being used centrally or laterally (see Figure 5.3). In practice, however, we only find lateral fricatives and lateral approximants (though see Chapter 8 for the lateral release of stops). In each case the air channel is situated at the side(s) of the tongue rather than medially over its centre. For example, the English [l] in 'lamp' is pronounced with the tongue tip against the alveolar ridge. However, the side rims of the tongue are lowered and so a channel is left, and air escapes through this channel (which may be either at the left, right or both sides of the tongue dependent on the speaker).

Figure 5.3 Lateral and median articulation

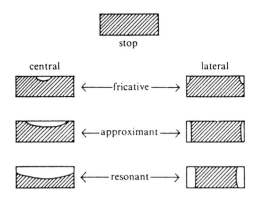

The four main stricture types are all prolongable, but there are other types that are momentary. We have already looked at the semi-vowel, which is a non-prolongable approximant. A non-prolongable stop is the *flap* (or 'tap') (see Figure 5.4). Like the stop, the flap involves a complete closure between two articulators; however, unlike the stop this is not held and the articulators part again rapidly (after between 10 to 20 msec). This means that air pressure does not built up to any extent behind the closure to produce plosion. One type of flap is the 'flick', where one articulator strikes another and then returns to its original position. This is the sound heard in some rather old-fashioned British English pronunciations of 'merry' ['meɾɪ], or American English pronunciations of 'city' ['sɪɾi]. The other type is the 'transient flap', where the moving articulator begins in one position but ends in another, e.g. [ɽ] in [saɽi], Hindi pronunciation of 'sari'. Some authorities give the name 'tap' to what we have called 'flick', and 'flap' to what we have called 'transient flap', and consider these as separate manners of articulation.

Finally we need to look at the *trill* category (see Figure 5.4). This is sometimes described as a series of flaps, but the frequency of articulator contacts suggests it is planned in a different way neurologically. A trill involves the rapid striking of one articulator against another (about 30 times a second). This requires, of course, one flexible articulator, and this appears to be restricted generally to the tongue tip and the uvula. Bilabial trills are possible, but have been reported very seldom.

We have been looking at all these manners of articulation in terms of a pulmonic egressive air flow. Looking at other air stream mechanisms we can note

Figure 5.4 Flaps and trills

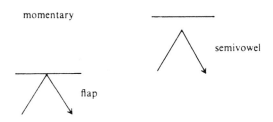

that clicks and implosives are stop like sounds, and these seem to be the only types possible on velaric and glottalic ingressive air flows respectively. The glottalic egressive air stream, on the other hand, is capable of producing many of the manners described above. We can find in natural languages, therefore, ejective stops, ejective fricatives and also ejective affricates (see Chapter 8 for a definition of affricates).

Disordered speech

In terms of disordered speech and articulation type, the main likelihood is an inability to produce one or more manner of articulation rather than the occurrence of novel stricture types (though of course speakers of a particular language may employ manners not normally found in that language).

One major problem is encountered with cleft palate patients and those with other forms of velopharyngeal inadequacy. This disorder often affects the ability to produce plosives, as air leakage through the nasal cavity stops the necessary build up of air pressure to make these sounds audible on release. Hypernasality may occur with all sound types, but this is discussed more fully in Chapter 7.

The only novel aspect of manners of articulation that might be encountered in the clinical situation is *reiteration*. Unlike simple prolongation, which is possible in many manners (and may also be found inappropriately in disordered speech), reiteration involves the unrequired (or abnormal) repetition of segments or syllables. There is usually no way of predicting which sounds will be susceptible to this repetition, as patients tend to display idiosyncratic behaviour in this respect. Reiteration is perhaps most associated with stuttering, but it can also occur with palilalia, and with Parkinson's disease acquired neurological disorders. Under PRDS conventions, this feature is shown by the use of superscript tie-bars: [k‿k‿k]. Developmental and acquired apraxia of speech, and dysarthria also often affect manner of articulation.

Further reading

Naturally, all text books in phonetics must devote a good deal of coverage to manners of articulation, and therefore perfectly adequate coverage is provided by, for example, Abercrombie (1967); Brosnahan and Malberg (1970); Ladefoged (1975); Dew and Jensen (1977), and briefer accounts are available in O'Connor (1973) and Denes and Pinson (1973). The very comprehensive collection on phonetics edited by Malmberg (1968) also contains information on this topic, while perhaps one of the best accounts is to be found in Catford (1977), with a somewhat more concise version in Catford (1988). In terms of disordered speech, the PRDS Group (1983) report obviously includes all the symbols referred to in this chapter, while Shriberg and Kent (1982) provide a more general discussion of disordered speech. For apraxia of speech, Miller (1986) is recommended, and for dysarthria, Netsell (1986).

CHAPTER 6

Place of Articulation

As we saw in the previous chapter, speech sounds (both normal and disordered) can be produced in a number of different 'manners'. However, for each of these manners the articulators may be in a variety of positions; that is to say there are also a number of places of articulation. In this chapter we will be looking at consonants only, and examining both the normal and non-normal places where they may be articulated.

As we made clear previously, the production of speech sounds requires the approximation of two articulators which interfere to a greater or lesser extent with the flow of air within the vocal tract. This approximation, or bringing together, can involve one static and one active articulator (e.g. tongue and hard palate) or two active articulators (e.g. the two lips). In this chapter we will look at the action of different articulators, or different parts of articulators.

Normal speech sounds

It is usual to describe the places of articulation in an anterior–posterior direction, i.e. working from the front of the oral cavity backwards, and we will follow this pattern. In normal speech no sounds are produced using articulators placed beyond the anterior boundary of the oral cavity; that is the two lips. We can start our examination therefore at this point.

Before we examine the different articulation locations, we need to look at a classification of the articulators involved. The most important of these are the lips, teeth and roof of the mouth, and the tongue. Figures 6.1 and 6.2 show the usual divisions and names of these, names we will encounter again in the terms given to the positions that two articulators can assume in speech.

Articulations involving the two lips as articulators are generally termed *bilabial* (see Figure 6.3). This name specifies both lower and upper articulator (bi: two; labial: lip), and as we will see, the full names of articulation positions all do this. Often, however, shortened forms exist, whereby the upper articulator only is named.

Figure 6.1 Divisions of the oral cavity

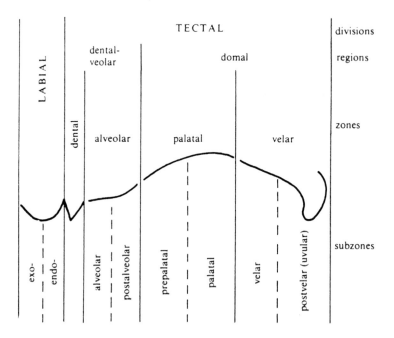

Figure 6.2 Divisions of the tongue

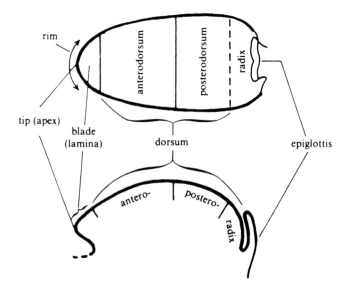

This is especially true for positions involving the tongue as the lower articulator. Therefore the term 'labial' is sometimes found for our first place of articulation. Readers should be cautious with this term, however, as it is also found as a general term for any articulation involving some use of lip position.

In a bilabial articulation, the lips are both active articulators. They approximate (or move towards each other) to produce, for example, stops (such as [b], [m]), or fricatives [ɸ], [β]. We will see in later chapters how a bilabial approximation also has a part to play in certain vowels and semi-vowel approximants.

Labiodental articulations can be considered next. The name of this articulation clearly shows that the lower articulator is the lower lip (labio-), while the upper one is the upper front teeth (-dental). The approximation of the lower lip to the upper teeth can be made to produce stops (such as [ɱ]), fricatives ([f, v]) or approximants ([ʋ]). The IPA has no symbols for labiodental oral stops, but they are known to occur in some languages (see Catford, 1977, pp. 147–8). To symbolize these, the IPA dental diacritic can be placed below the [p, b] symbols: [p̪, b̪] (see also Disordered Speech below).

With both bilabial and labiodental articulations we can, if we wish, specify further the lip shape. While this is rarely important for normal speech, it may be so for disordered. The terms endolabial and exolabial (respectively inner and outer surface of the lip) can be used for both upper and lower lips in bilabial articulation, and for the lower lip in labiodental articulation. For example, a 'voiceless endolabial–dental fricative' describes [f] pronounced with the inner part of the lower lip articulating with the lower edge of the upper front teeth. This is the normal pronunciation of English [f]. On the other hand the approximant [ʋ] is often pronounced exolabially.

Most of the remaining places of articulation involve some part of the tongue as the active articulator, and some part of the roof of the mouth as the passive articulator. We will be examining only the common articulations of normal speech (Catford, 1977, pp. 148f describes some very unusual ones, some of which we describe in Disordered Speech below).

In these articulations, the lower (and active) articulator is the tongue, and as we saw in Figure 6.2, it can be divided into 'sections'. The names of these sections provide prefixes which are sometimes used with the following places of articulation. Although we introduce the full forms here for reference purposes, we will generally use the shorter forms in this book.

The *apicodental* place of articulation involves the tip of the tongue articulating against the rims or backs of the upper front teeth. Amongst the sounds produced here are stops (e.g. [n̪] [t̪]), lateral approximants ([l̪]) and trills ([r̪]). Fricatives, too, can be produced, but here the channel shape (see Chapter 5) has a part to play. The wide-channel fricatives ([θ], [ð]) are sometimes pronounced with the tongue tip protruding between upper and lower teeth, and so are often termed 'interdental'. The narrow-channel fricatives ([s̪], [z̪] can be apicodental, but are not found with interdental articulation.

Figure 6.3 Examples of place of articulation: bilabial, alveolar, palatal, velar

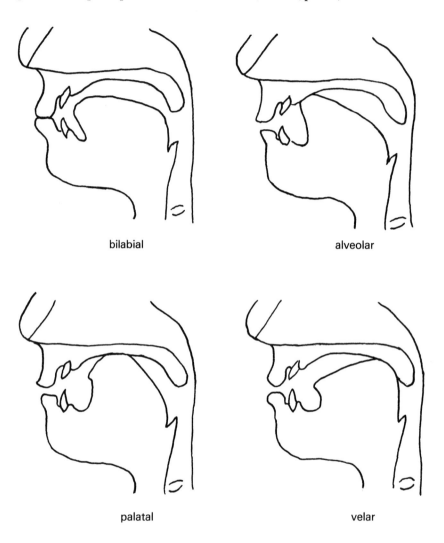

bilabial

alveolar

palatal

velar

The alveolar (or tooth) ridge is the passive articulator against which tip or blade articulation of the tongue can be made (see Figure 6.3). The difference between *apicoalveolar* and *laminoalveolar* is auditorily very slight, and difficult to notice visually. In many cases it appears that the choice between these two varies from individual to individual for any language, or even from occasion to occasion for one speaker (see Bladon and Nolan, 1977). For all these reasons, the difference between these two forms of alveolar articulation is not marked in transcription.

In producing alveolar consonants, the tongue tip or blade is brought up to articulate with the flat part of the alveolar ridge immediately behind the upper front teeth. For blade articulations, the tongue tip may be in contact with the back of the upper front teeth. Stops, fricatives, approximants, trills and taps can all be produced at this place (e.g. [n, t, z, l, r, ɾ]. The IPA has no diacritic to mark alveolar place.

Apicopostalveolar is a variant of the preceding place, in which the tongue articulates against the back part of the alveolar ridge (resulting in a degree of bending upwards of the tongue apex). The typical British English /r/ (=[ɹ]) in words like 'rain' and /tr/ (=[t̠ɹ]) as in 'train' have a postalveolar articulation. Whereas some authorities use the term (lamino–) postalveolar for the fricatives [ʃ,ʒ], in this book they are classed as palatoalveolars, and are described below.

Although the term *retroflex* is abandoned by some leading phoneticians (e.g. Catford, 1977), it has such a wide and lengthy currency that it has been retained here. It should be noted, however, that it is unlike the other terms in referring to tongue shape rather than position along the roof of the mouth. Retroflex articulations are typically apical or sublaminal (i.e. using the underside of the tongue blade), involving a postalveolar or, perhaps more usually, a prepalatal position. To make a retroflex approximation the tip of the tongue is raised to touch, or come close to, one of these positions. In doing so, the tip is actually bent backwards to a greater or lesser degree, dependent on language and speaker. Stops, fricatives, approximants, and flaps all occur in retroflex mode, e.g. (ɳ, ɖ, ʂ, ɭ, ɽ].[1]

Laminopalato-alveolar articulations involve an approximation of the blade of the tongue with the alveolar ridge and the hard palate (usually the front part of the hard palate). The sounds characteristically produced in this way are the narrow channel fricatives [ʃ] and [ʒ].[2]

The next four places of articulation are all dorsal, in that the dorsum of the tongue is involved. In traditional terms the first two involve the front (antedorsum) and the second two the back (postdorsum) of the tongue.

Dorsoalveolo-palatal (or dorsoprepalatal) articulations involve the front part of the tongue approximating to the forward arch of the hard palate. While many kinds of consonants may be articulated here, IPA symbols are only provided for the fricatives ([ɕ, ʑ]), which are found in Polish written as ś, ź, Should other alveolo-palatal symbols be required, the relevant palatal symbols can be used together with the diacritic mark for 'advanced place': [₊].

Dorsopalatal position involves an articulation of the front of the tongue with the main part of the hard palate (see Figure 6.3). Stops, fricatives, and approximants can all be made with this articulation, e.g. [ɲ, ɟ, ç, ʎ].

Dorsovelar articulations involve the approximation of the back of the tongue to the velum (or soft palate) (see Figure 6.3). This position is often subject to a certain degree of advancement or retraction in certain languages. This is often due to the influence of neighbouring sounds. For example, the velar stop [k] in English 'key' is advanced under the influence of the front [i] (this is shown in transcription by writing [k̟]), whereas the [k] in 'car' is retracted due to the influence of the back

Table 6.1. Symbols for Normal Speech

		Bilabial	Labio-dental	Dental	Alveolar	Post-alveolar	Retro-flex	Palato-alveolar	Alveolo-palatal	Palatal	Velar	Uvular	Pharyn-geal	Glottal
Stop	nasal	m	ɱ	n̪	n		ɳ			ɲ	ŋ	ɴ		
	plosive	p b		t̪ d̪	t d		ʈ ɖ			c ɟ	k g	q ɢ		ʔ
Fricative	median	ɸ β	f v	θ ð	s	ɹ̝	ʂ ʐ	ʃ ʒ	ɕ ʑ	ç ʝ	x ɣ	χ ʁ	ħ ʕ	h ɦ
	lateral			ɬ̪ ɮ̪	ɬ ɮ		ɭ̥							
Approximant	median		ʋ			ɹ	ɻ			j	ɰ			
	lateral			l̪	l		ɭ			ʎ	ʟ			
Trill				r̪	r		ɽ̃					ʀ		
Tap/flap				r̪	ɾ		ɽ							
Ejective		p'		t̪'	t'					k'				
Implosive		ɓ		ɗ̪	ɗ					ɠ	ʛ			
Click	median	ʘ		ʇ	ʇ	ʗ								
	lateral			ʖ	ʖ									

vowel [ɑ] (transcribed as [k̲]). Stops, fricatives and approximants are found in velar position, e.g. [ŋ, g, x, ɰ].

Dorsouvular articulations are formed by an approximation of the back and/or root of the tongue with the extreme end of the velum, including the uvula. Stops and fricatives can occur at this place, e.g. [N, q, ɢ, χ, ʀ]. Also there occurs the uvular trill, [ʙ], which is made slighly differently, by allowing the uvula to trill in an egressive air flow.

The remaining two traditional places of articulation — pharyngeal and glottal — will only be described briefly here, though Catford (1977) shows that a more detailed description is needed to account for some rare speech sounds. Pharyngeal place of articulation covers any constriction to the air flow occurring in the pharynx. This may result from retraction of the tongue root, or lateral compression of the oropharynx. As primary articulations, only pharyngeal fricatives occur in normal speech: [ħ, ʕ].

Glottal articulations are taken here to refer to the traditional terms of glottal stop and fricative (see Catford, 1977, pp. 163-4 for description of the rare ventricular sounds of some Caucasian languages). The articulators involved are the vocal folds, brought together for the glottal stop ([ʔ], but slightly apart for the fricatives, [h, ɦ]. In effect, [ɦ] the voiced glottal fricative, is an example of the 'whispery voice' phonation type (see Chapter 3), and the voiceless glottal fricative [h] is a voiceless onset to the following vowel. It can be argued, too, that the glottal stop is in reality a phonation type (see Chapter 3) rather than, or as well as, a sound segment.

This survey of place types does not include double or secondary articulations which are described in Chapter 10. We can review our work on both place and manner of articulation in normal speech in the chart shown in Table 6.1.

Disordered speech

Disordered speech does not of course imply that the sounds involved are outside the range normally found in speech. Often the disorder is an organizational one, or is one including normal speech sounds but ones that are outside the range for the language in question.

However, there are a range of non-normal places of articulation that are encountered in the clinic. A variety of disorders may present that use some or all of these, including developmental or acquired apraxia of speech, dysarthria, and specific learning disability.

PRDS has provided a set of symbols for these places of articulation, and they can be broken down into two main groups: totally novel articulation places, and those that are only novel for a particular manner of articulation. The first group includes 'lingualabials' (tongue tip/blade to upper lip), 'reverse labiodentals' (lower teeth to upper lip), and 'bidentals' (lower and upper teeth together) (see Figure 6.4). In the second group we find bilabial trills, labiodental plosives, interdentals, a voiced velar lateral, and pharyngeal plosives.

Table 6.2. Symbols for Disordered Speech

	Bilabial	Lingua labial	Labiodental	Reverse Labiodental	Interdental	Bidental	Palatal	Velar	Pharyngeal
Plosive	p b	p b	p̪ b̪	p̺ b̺	t̪⁺ d̪⁺				q̠ ɢ̠
Nasal		m	m̪	m̺	n̪⁺				
Fricative	ɸ β		f̪ v̪	f̺ v̺		h̪ ɦ̪	j		
Percussive						͜ʖ			
Lateral approximant		ʟ						ʟ̠	
Trill	͡ppp bbb								

Figure 6.4 Examples of non-normal articulation: lingualabial, reverse labiodental, bidental

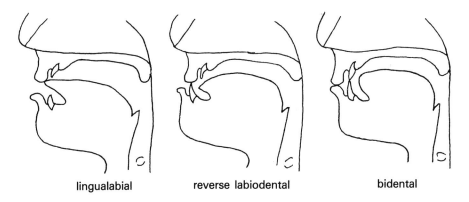

lingualabial	reverse labiodental	bidental

Several new diacritics and symbols are also suggested for articulations which, although not non-normal, occur often in the clinic and lack clear IPA symbolization. These are a symbol for the voiced palatal fricative ([ʝ], leaving [j] for the approximant), and diacritics for alveolar slit (as opposed to grooved) fricatives ([θ̠] and [ð̠]), and for blade as opposed to tip articulations at alveolar place (e.g. [s̪]). The PRDS symbols for non-normal places of articulation are given in Table 6.2 below.

Further reading

What was said in the equivalent section of the previous chapter applies equally here. In effect, all phonetics books go into some detail on place of articulation, with the Catford (1977) book providing perhaps the best coverage. Shriberg and Kent (1982) and PRDS Group (1983) both discuss aspects of disordered speech, and Ball (1988a) provides a critique of many of the PRDS symbol proposals.

Notes

1. Also transcribed as [n̪, d̪, s̪, l̪, r̪].
2. In US usage these are usually transcribed [š] and [ž].

CHAPTER 7

Orality and Nasality

We discussed briefly in Chapter 5 the fact that the stop manner of articulation was divisible into two sub-types: nasals and plosives. We will have more to say about plosives in the next chapter, but here we will examine more closely the notion of nasality.

Technically speaking, the term nasality should not be used as a manner of articulation, as all manners of articulation are capable of being pronounced orally (i.e. with the velum raised) or nasally (with the velum lowered). It just happens that for consonants the manner of articulation most commonly found pronounced nasally is the stop category. For this reason, when phoneticians use the label nasal by itself, they are usually referring to nasal stops.

As noted, nasality or orality in speech is a reflection of the physical position of the velum, or soft palate. We saw in Chapter 1 that the velum can be raised to block off the nasal cavity from the oral cavity (and therefore from a pulmonic egressive air flow), or lowered to allow the egressive air to flow through the nasal cavity. However, the use of the terms 'raised' or 'lowered' suggests a simple dichotomy (as of course do the labels 'oral' and 'nasal'), and this is not really the case. As we will see, various degrees of velar raising/lowering are possible, leading to different degrees of nasality. This distinction is not always necessary to observe strictly in the description of normal speech, but it can be so in non-normal speech.

A further distinction made by phoneticians revolves around whether a sound pronounced with lowered velum involves the oral cavity as well as the nasal, or simply the latter. Sounds pronounced via the nasal cavity alone are generally termed 'nasal', whereas those involving both cavities are termed 'nasalized'. We will exemplify this distinction below (see Figure 7.1).

Normal speech

Fully nasal (as opposed to nasalized) sounds occur in normal speech only when the oral cavity has been blocked by an articulator, thus leaving the nasal cavity as the

38

only exit for an egressive air flow (see Figure 7.1). Naturally, it is only the stop consonants which have the characteristic of fully blocking the oral cavity. Nasal stops are thus produced by a full constriction between articulators somewhere in the oral cavity, together with a lowered velum. They can be produced at many places of articulation (though not pharyngeal or glottal, as these are outside the oral cavity). The following are the IPA symbols employed for nasal stops: [m, ɱ, n, ɳ, ɲ, ŋ, ɴ].

It will be noticed that, whereas the IPA provides voiceless and voiced symbols for oral stops or plosives, voiced symbols alone are provided for nasal stops. This should not be taken to imply that voiceless nasals do not occur in attested languages: they occur, for example, in Thai and Burmese. However, they are relatively uncommon, perhaps because of the lack of intensity found with such sounds. They can be transcribed using the IPA's diacritic for voicelessness, [̥], [m̥, n̥, ŋ̥]. In order to increase the intensity of voiceless nasals, and to add further acoustic cues to their place of articulation, these sounds often occur with a short voiced nasal segment following them, for example: [və ŋ̊ŋɑr], *fy nghar*, 'my car', in one variety of Welsh.

As we saw above, other manners of articulation can also be pronounced with a fully or partially lowered velum. However, these are best described as nasalized, as there is no complete closure in the oral cavity. Therefore for these sounds both oral and nasal cavities are in use (see Figure 7.1).

Nasalized fricatives or approximants are rarely encountered in normal speech, though Catford (1977, p. 147) notes nasalized [ṽ] as occurring in English as an allophone (i.e. variant) of /m/ in words like 'triumph'. The same sound, [ṽ], is reported in some Welsh dialects (see Jones, 1984, p. 51), and is believed to have been a major sound (or 'phoneme') of that language in its early form. To mark any of these consonants as nasalized, it is necessary to utilize the IPA's nasalization diacritic: [̃], e.g. [l̃, ṽ].

The most common group of nasalized sounds are the vowels. Indeed, most languages have occasions when vowels become nasalized to some extent (see discussion on this below), and many have nasalized vowels as distinctive phonemes, contrasting with oral vowels. Many readers will be familiar with the nasalized vowels of French, where up to four such are found phonemically: [œ̃, ɛ̃, ɑ̃, õ], though [œ̃] is lacking in some accents. Again, it will be noticed that the diacritic for nasalization (called 'tilde') is added to the vowel symbol in transcription.

We will turn our attention now to one last group of sounds where nasalization is common, although the sounds themselves are rare enough: *clicks*. In reality, the so-called nasal clicks are really double articulations (see Chapter 10), but we can briefly refer to them here. As was noted in Chapter 2, the air-stream mechanism used in producing clicks is initiated at the velum. This means that the velum may be raised or lowered and clicks can still be produced. If the velum is lowered, pulmonic egressive air can flow out through the nasal cavity simultaneously with the click production; thus a combined click and nasal is heard. Depending on the place of articulation of the click (the nasal is always velar, of course), these sounds can be transcribed as [ĩŋ], [ʃ̃ŋ] and so on.

Figure 7.1 Nasal, oral and nasalized

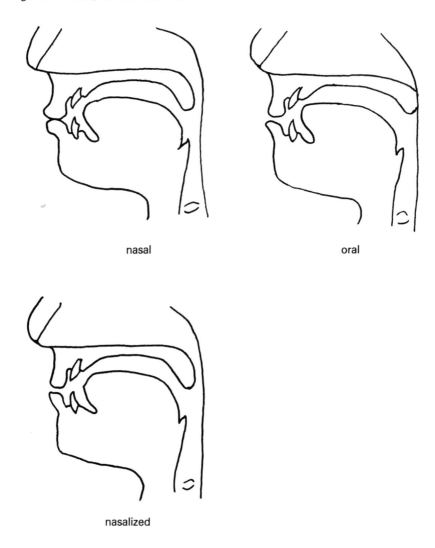

nasal

oral

nasalized

To conclude this section we will look at degrees of nasality. The raising and the lowering of the velum is a physical activity which takes a finite amount of time and involves a finite amount of space. Taking the first point: as the lowering of the velum is not instantaneous, an increasing amount of nasality occurs during the lowering until it is fully lowered when we perceive 'full' nasality. Conversely, a decreasing amount of nasality is perceived during the time it takes to raise the velum again after a nasal(ized) sound. This is why the quality of vowels in the environment of a nasal stop can be perceived as nasalized to some degree, even if the language in question lacks nasalized vowel phonemes. In English, the vowel [æ] in 'map' and in 'Pam' is to some extent nasalized: the first 'prenasalized' and the second 'postnasalized'. These can be transcribed as [mⁿæp], [pæⁿm] in a very narrow transcription, though [mǽp], [pǽm] is often sufficient. In a broad transcription, this nasalization can be assumed to be deducible by the reader from the context, and so omitted.

In terms of the extent of velar lowering, it is quite common to find that the velum is not fully raised during oral speech, or fully lowered during nasal speech. Many normal speakers are slightly over- or undernasal (also termed hyper- and hyponasal) in their speech, either all the time or at certain times or in certain phonetic environments. It is not normally necessary to transcribe these features, though Canepari (1983) suggests transcriptions such as [a̰] for slight nasalization. Unfortunately, other phoneticians use the 'subscript tilde' to denote pharyngealization (see Chapter 10) or creak/creaky voice (see Chapter 3), and these usages are referenced in Pullum and Ladusaw (1987).

Disordered speech

Hypernasality in speech is a common occurrence with speakers with velopharyngeal inadequacy caused by cleft palate or neurological impairment. Some speakers who are hypernasal may also produce nasal friction: that is an audible and turbulent nasal air flow. This may be used as an attempt to signal fricatives, but with some patients it may be ever present or randomly present. With patients of this type, it is important that the distinction between a nasal and a nasalized sound discussed above is observed. For example, as an attempt at fricative articulation, one patient may produce a nasalized fricative (e.g. [s̃], while another might produce a nasal fricative with *no* oral escape (e.g. [ŋᶠ]).

For any nasalized sound, the diacritic [˜] is used. The use of [̰] for slight nasalization is noted above but is perhaps best avoided for the reasons noted. Pre- and postnasalization can be transcribed in the ways already noted. Oral stop symbols with the tilde diacritic stand for sounds intermediate between oral and nasal stops: [t̃], [p̃], and so on. For any sound with nasal friction as defined above the diacritic [ᶠ] is recommended (e.g. [mᶠ], [ŋ̊ᶠ]. For fully nasal sounds, the ordinary nasal stop symbols (with voiceless diacritic when necessary) should be sufficient.

Hyponasality generally presents few problems for transcription. If target nasal sounds are fully denasalized, then oral stop symbols can be used. If they are partially denasalized then the symbols for sounds between oral and nasal stops (e.g. [b̃], [d̃]) can be utilized.

Further reading

Many accounts of phonetics do not examine the oral – nasal – nasality distinction in any detail, though Brosnahan and Malmberg (1970) are notable exceptions in the treatment devoted to the area in their chapter 6. A good introduction to the study of cleft palate is given in Crystal (1980, pp. 187f), and the standard works in the area are Morley (1970), Holdsworth (1970) and Ross and Johnston (1972). The various transcriptional recommendations are based on IPA and PRDS norms.

CHAPTER 8

Plosive Theory

We examined stop consonants previously in Chapter 5, but as oral stops can be modified in several different ways, it is necessary to look at them in more detail. This chapter, then, examines the various ways in which the articulation of pulmonic egressive oral stops can be adapted.

Normal speech

The three phases of the stop

Plosive stop consonants can be considered to consist of three phases: firstly the 'shutting phase', then the 'closure phase', and finally the 'release phase'.

The *shutting phase* is that during which the relevant articulators come together to create a complete stop against the air flow. This is followed by a length of time (approximately 50–60 msec) during which the articulators are kept closed. This *closure phase* is in fact a period of silence for voiceless stops, and simply the vocal cord 'buzz' for fully voiced stops. Although the closure phase is comparatively short, it is long enough for air pressure to build up. This means that when the articulators move apart again in the *release phase*, this movement is accompanied by the equalization of air pressure differences. We hear this as the characteristic 'popping' noise that gives the plosive its name as the air rushes out on release of the stop.

In many languages (including English), modifications can occur to phase 1 or phase 3 of the stop. Phase 2 is always present, despite its relative lack of perceptual strength. For this reason, stops are classified in terms of where the closure stage takes place, and modifications to other stages are noted only as secondary characteristics.

43

Stops and velic action

The release phase of a stop may be transferred from oral release to nasal release (see Figure 8.1). This must not be confused with what happens in a nasal stop. Nasal stops have a lowered velum throughout the sound, whereas a nasally released stop requires the velum to be lowered only at the final phase. Phase 3, then, sees the lowering of the velum, but the articulators remain in the same place. This means that the stop is perceived to be followed by a homorganic nasal (nasal of the same place of articulation).

In phonetic transcription, we generally note nasal release (sometimes termed 'nasal plosion') simply by the use of the oral plosive symbol followed by the nasal stop symbol: [sʌbmə'rin], 'submarine'. However, if it is required to stress the nasal release feature, a superscript capital-N can be employed: [bᴺ]. As noted in Chapter 4, nasals can sometimes act as syllabic nuclei, and in English this is found with these nasally released segments (though not all nasally released stops are syllabic nuclei): ['bʌtn̩], 'button'.

Figure 8.1 Nasal release

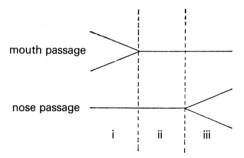

It is possible also to modify the shutting phase of a stop to velic action. In this event, the coming together of articulators co-occurs with a lowering of the velum. Therefore, a nasal stop is produced. However, instead of this nasal stop being resolved in the normal way, the velum is then raised to produce an oral stop. This in turn can be released with normal oral plosion. This 'nasal approach' (see Figure 8.2) again involves homorganic nasal and oral, and can be seen in English in words such as ['ʌndə], 'under', [lʌmp], 'lump' and [hænd], 'hand'.

The transference of both phase 1 and phase 3 is also possible. In effect the process here involves the formation of a nasal stop with an oral segment in the middle (see Figure 8.3). The articulators come together with a simultaneous lowering of the velum. The articulators remain in the same place while the velum is raised and then lowered again to create what we perceive as an intervening oral stop. As the articulators do not move, all three 'segments' are homorganic. Examples of stops with nasal approach and nasal release are found in ['stæmpməʃin], 'stampmachine' and [sənt'nɪkələs], 'Saint Nicholas'.

Figure 8.2 Nasal approach

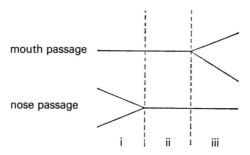

Figure 8.3 Nasal approach and nasal release

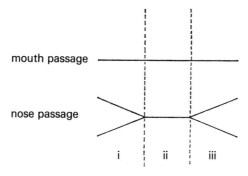

Stops with lateral release

As we have seen, stops may have oral or nasal plosion. If the plosion is oral, its release may be central or lateral. Central plosion occurs if there is a central passage in the vocal tract for air released in phase 3. It is possible, however, to maintain the articulatory closure centrally, but by lowering the side rims of the tongue to create a lateral passage down which plosion occurs. We perceive this as a stop followed by a homorganic lateral, and it is generally transcribed by the use of the relevant plosive symbol, followed by a lateral: ['bædlı], 'badly'. If need be, to show explicitly lateral release, a superscript capital-L can be employed: [dᴸ]. As with the case of syllabic-n, laterals can also act as syllabic nuclei. This occurs in many accents of English, as in ['lɪtl̩], 'little', ['mɪdl̩], 'middle', and so on.

Incomplete stops

Another modification of plosives can occur through the suppression of plosion itself at phase 3. In other words, the necessary articulatory movements are made, but the suppressed air is not audibly released. This occurs in two main instances. Firstly, it can occur if one plosive is followed immediately by another. In some languages (e.g. French) the second stops shutting phase is not completed until the first stop has been released; therefore two separate plosion periods are heard. In other languages (e.g. English), the closure phase of the second stop commences before the release of the first stop can take place. The first stop here is therefore incomplete (see Figure 8.4).

Examples from English include [æp˺tʰ], 'apt', and [ˈæk˺tʰə], 'actor'. If the two stops are homorganic and of the same voicing, then in reality what we have is simply an extra long closure stage in a single stop; so 'bookcase' can be transcribed either as [ˈbʊk˺kʰeɪs], or [ˈbʊkːeɪs].

The second instance of incomplete stops occurs in certain languages when a stop is word final. For example, in English, the 'p' in the word 'stop' itself may be pronounced with plosion, [stɒpʰ], or with no audible release, [stɒp˺].

Figure 8.4a Complete stop sequences

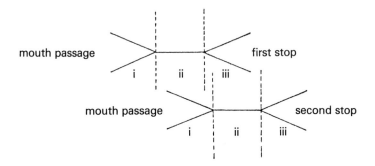

Figure 8.4b Incomplete stop sequences

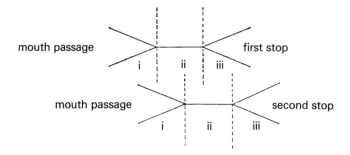

Affrication

Affrication is a further way of modifying the release phase of a plosive. Whereas normally the articulators move relatively widely apart to facilitate the outrush of compressed air, in an affricated stop the articulators move only slightly apart, leaving a narrow channel (see Figure 8.5). Thus the escaping air is perceived as friction, and an affricated stop is usually transcribed with a stop symbol followed by a superscript fricative symbol: [tˢ], [kˣ]. If the stop and fricative parts of the sound are approximately of equal strength, we call the resulting sound an 'affricate' English affricates are the sounds [t͡ʃ] and [d͡ʒ] (or [ʧ] and [ʤ], or simply [tʃ] and [dʒ][1]), as in 'church' and 'judge'.

Figure 8.5 Affrication

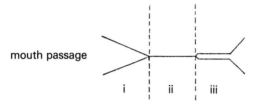

Aspiration

The final phase 3 feature that we will examine concerns the coordination of stop release and vocal fold vibration. In a fully voiced stop, vocal fold vibration takes place throughout all stages of the stop. In a voiceless stop, however, voicing can commence for the following sound (assuming it is voiced) immediately on release of plosion, or following a period of voicelessness (see Figure 8.6). This 'voice onset time' (VOT) varies from language to language (or even between types of stop in any one language). We term the sound quality of this period of voicelessness 'aspiration', and it is usually transcribed as superscript-h. In English, most voiceless stops are aspirated, with a VOT of about 60–70 msec. Following 's' however, English voiceless stops are unaspirated, therefore we can distinguish 'peak' [pʰikʰ] from 'speak' [sp⁼ikʰ].

Figure 8.6 Aspiration

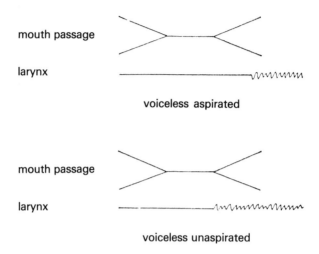

mouth passage

larynx

voiceless aspirated

mouth passage

larynx

voiceless unaspirated

Disordered speech

As we have noted in other chapters, various disorders may prevent the production of some or all of the stop types we have described here. This may be due to articulatory problems (e.g. dysarthria), or to higher level organizational deficits. However, in terms of plosives, particular problems occur with cleft palate and similar patients, and these were discussed in Chapter 7. Apart from these, difficulties can occur in particular with the various fine controls needed in the modifications to the basic stop type.

We find, therefore, epenthetic vowels inserted between stop and nasal to avoid nasal release, and lateral vocalization to avoid lateral release. These are particularly common in disordered child phonology, giving us forms like ['bʌtən] for ['bʌtn̩], 'button', or ['mɪdʊ] for ['mɪdl̩], 'middle'. Though it should be noted that these forms are acceptable in some accents. Problems also occur in the mastering of affricates, which may be replaced by stops in many forms of speech disorder (less commonly by fricatives). Finally, aspiration may not be properly mastered, leading to confusions between fortis and lenis stops.

Further reading

The most comprehensive accounts of plosive theory are to be found in Abercrombie (1967) chapter 9, and Ladefoged (1975) chapter 6, pp. 124f. Wells and Colson

(1971) devote a chapter (chapter 16) to plosive theory, from the particular viewpoint of practical phonetics. As noted in previous chapters, PRDS and IPA conventions have been used in transcriptions. Crystal (1980) provides an introduction to disorders like dysarthria and childhood articulatory problems mentioned in the final section.

---

1. In US usage these are transcribed as [č] and [ǰ].

CHAPTER 9

Vowels

Vowels are not as easy to classify as consonants. The main reason for this is that the vowel (or resonant) manner of articulation requires a wide articulatory channel, thus resulting in no contact or near contact between the articulators. Therefore, terms like alveolar, palatal, velar etc., are generally not found to describe vowel sounds.

Traditionally, a set of articulatory parameters have been utilized to describe vowels. These cover three 'dimensions':

1. highest point of the 'tongue-arch' on the vertical axis;
2. highest point of the tongue-arch on the horizontal axis;
3. lip shape.

The possible sub-divisions of each dimension are as follows:

a. close (= closest to palate), half-close, half-open, open; alternative labels are high, half-high, half-low, low, although some phoneticians only use three points: high, mid, low;
b. front, mid (or central), back; though often simply front and back will be used;
c. rounded, neutral, spread; or simply rounded and unrounded.

These terms are only useful as a rough guide to vowel quality, however. Due to the relatively open articulatory channel with vowels, the tongue is able to move slightly from position to position, producing a near infinity of different vowel qualities. Our limited number of terms, then, can never be expected to describe these thoroughly.

The Cardinal Vowel System

Primary cardinal vowels

As an attempt to solve the problem of vowel description, the famous British phonetician, Daniel Jones, devised the Cardinal Vowel System around the time of the

First World War. This is a system of fixed auditory reference points (like the points of the compass) to which any vowel sound can be related in a principled manner.

Jones' Cardinal Vowel System is designed around eight primary cardinal vowels. These were chosen on an arbitrary basis (in that they are not designed to be the vowels of any particular language), but they are planned also (in that they aim to be auditorily equidistant and to give comprehensive coverage of the vowel area).

In drawing up his Cardinal Vowel System, Jones paid attention to the vowel area: that is the area within the oral cavity where vowel sounds can be produced. The boundaries of this area are relatively easy to ascertain: in many respects it is not possible to move the tongue further (e.g. the lower boundary of the floor of the mouth); elsewhere, moving the tongue too high will result in the production of approximant or fricative sounds. The vowel area is shown in Figure 9.1. It should be remembered that, with the exception of certain retroflexed vowels, the shape of the tongue when vowels are produced is 'humped', i.e. convex.

Figure 9.1 The vowel area

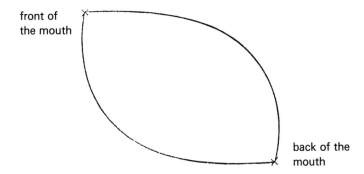

Jones chose to position his eight reference vowels around the outside of this vowel area, as he felt that peripheral vowels would be most convenient. The placing of the vowels can be considered in three stages. The first of these stages sees the establishment of two cardinal vowels on articulatory criteria to act as 'anchors' to the whole system. The first of these (numbered Cardinal Vowel 1, or CV1) was created by Jones to be the highest, frontest vowel he could make without the sound becoming consonantal. The second of these anchors (numbered CV5) was created by Jones to be the lowest, backest vowel he could make while still being vocalic. Both of these were made with spread lips.

The second stage consisted of inserting three more reference points along the periphery of the forward part of the vowel area between CV1 and CV5. The space between each of these five cardinal vowels (numbered CV1-5) was judged to be auditorily (though not necessarily articulatory) equidistant. CVs 1–5 are all pronounced with spread lips.

Figure 9.2 Primary cardinal vowels

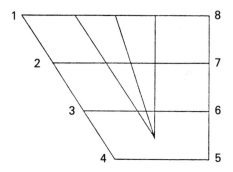

C.V. One: i; C.V. Two: e; C.V. Three: ɛ; C.V. Four: a; C.V. Five: ɑ; C.V. Six: ɔ; C.V. Seven: o; C.V. Eight: u.

The final stage consists of inserting three more cardinal vowels along the peripherary of the backward part of the vowel area, between CV5 and CV1. CVs 6–8 are again auditorily equidistant, but are pronounced with rounded lips. It should be noted that lip-rounding becomes progressively tighter the closer the vowel is. All the CVs can be seen in Figure 9.2 where they are placed on the conventional form of the vowel diagram. As you will see from this Figure, the IPA provides eight vowel symbols to stand for the eight primary cardinal vowels: [i, e, ɛ, a, ɑ, ɔ, o, u].

The Cardinal Vowel System is used as an auditory reference system. The user must have learnt the auditory quality of each cardinal vowel from a competent teacher, or from an acceptable recording (Jones made several of these himself). Then, when the user wishes to describe any vowel of any language they can classify it in terms of how near it is to a particular cardinal vowel (diacritics are available to show differences from cardinal quality in symbolic form: see the final section of this chapter). Verbally, such relationships are described in terms of a particular vowel sounding 'higher, fronter, more rounded' etc, than the nearest cardinal vowel. This is unfortunate terminology, perhaps, as it suggests the system is an articulatory one, when in fact it is mainly auditory.

Secondary cardinal vowels

While claiming that the primary cardinal vowels are all that are needed to describe the vowels of natural language, Jones recognized that many phoneticians would require a fuller system. To this end he created also a set of secondary cardinal vowels. The first eight of these (CVs 9–16) are simply the primary cardinal vowels with reversed lip-rounding. That is to say, whereas 1–5 are unrounded, 9–13 are rounded; and whereas 6–8 are rounded, 14–16 are unrounded. The symbols for 9–16 are: [y, ø, œ, Œ, ɒ, ʌ, ɤ, ɯ,]. These are shown on Figure 9.3.

The remaining six secondary cardinal vowels are not all peripheral, and provide reference points for central vowels. There are three pairs of these (each pair representing unrounded/rounded), respectively in close, half-close and half-open positions (see Figure 9.3). The symbols for 17–22 are: [ɨ, ʉ, ə, ɵ, ɜ, ɞ]. Some authorities recognize only 17 and 18, and use [ə] as a general cover symbol for all non-peripheral central vowels.

Apart from these twenty-two cardinal vowel symbols, the IPA provide a set of 'spare' vowel symbols often used to transcribe lax vowels in a language ('lax' as opposed to 'tense' vowels are pronounced with less muscular effort, tend to be short and centralized: compare tense 'leap' with lax 'lip'). The spare symbols for front vowels are: high unrounded [ɪ]/[ɪ], high rounded [ʏ], low [æ]; for central vowels: [ə] (generally called 'schwa'), [ɐ]; for back vowels: [ɒ]/[ʊ].

Figure 9.3 Secondary cardinal vowels

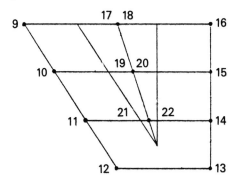

C.V. Nine: y; C.V. Ten: ø; C.V. Eleven: œ; C.V. Twelve: Œ; C.V. Thirteen: ɒ; C.V. Fourteen: ʌ; C.V. Fifteen: ɤ; C.V. Sixteen: ɯ; C.V. Seventeen: ɨ; C.V. Eighteen: ʉ; C.V. Nineteen: ə; C.V. Twenty: ɵ; C.V. Twenty-one: ɜ; C.V. Twenty-two: ɞ .

Criticisms of Cardinal Vowel Theory

The main criticism of the theory is found in the mixing of articulatory and auditory criteria. As we have seen, the creation of the system was partly articulatory (CVs 1 and 5), and partly auditory (CVs 2–4, 6–8). In its use it is primarily a way of recording auditory impressions, but these are couched in articulatory terms.

Secondly, the use of the system depends largely on how well you are taught, and how good an 'ear' you have. Ladefoged's (1967) experiment demonstrated how far 'off the track' even trained phoneticians can get when confronted with unusual vowel sounds.

Finally, the division between unrounded and rounded CVs appears somewhat strange (though it does reflect the usual European — and particularly English — preference). However, without recourse to experimental procedures, the system is probably the best we have for the description of vowel qualities.

It is also worth noting that in recent times some phoneticians have raised objections to the whole 'tongue-arch' model of vowel production as outlined at the beginning of this chapter, and have proposed a radically different model whereby vowels are described in terms of four places of articulation: palatal, velar, upper pharyngeal and lower pharyngeal. Wood (e.g. 1982) is the leading proponent of this view, but at least at the moment, while having much to recommend it, this approach has not been widely adopted.

Diphthongs

Diphthongs are vocalic segments where the tongue moves during the production of the vowel so that the quality at the end of the segment is different from that at the beginning. They are not the same as sequences of two contiguous vowels (as in 'naive') because, firstly, diphthongs are pronounced on one syllable, not two, and secondly, despite their name, there are not just two qualities involved, but a whole range as the tongue slides from the initial position to the final one. Despite this fact, diphthongs are generally symbolized by giving their initial and final position vowel symbols, e.g: [ɑʊ], [iə], [eɪ] etc. Sometimes the final symbols demonstrate an 'ideal' final position that is not always reached by every speaker or in every context.

Diphthongs can be classified according to where on the vowel diagram the final part of the segment is, so we can have 'closing', 'opening' or 'centring' diphthongs. Another classification concerns whether the initial or final segment holds the main stress or length of the diphthong. Under this system we have 'falling diphthongs' with the stress on the first element, and 'rising diphthongs' with the stress on the last element.

It is sometimes claimed that some accents of English have 'triphthongs' as in 'fire' ([faɪə]) and 'hour' ([ɑʊə]). For most speakers these are in fact either diphthongs with the loss of the middle quality ([faə] and [ɑə]), or bisyllabic, that is to say diphthongs + [ə].

Disordered speech

Studies of phonological disorders often ignore disruption to the vowel system. This should not be taken to mean that such disruptions do not occur. However, because of the impossibility of producing vowels outside the boundaries of the vowel area, we do not encounter new places or types of vowels that cannot be found in normal speech. Often differences that do occur may be in terms of loss of vowel units from the system, or changes in the phonetic quality of vowels. All these can be captured through the cardinal vowel system and diacritical symbols. Other features, such as nasality (Chapter 7) and excessively short or long vowels (Chapter 11) are dealt with elsewhere in this book.

Recently, some of the new phonological assessment procedures that have been developed for speech pathology have recognized that vowels can be affected in disordered speech and have made provision for recording them. The most important examples of these is Crystal's (1982) PROPH ('Profile in Phonology').

Diacritics

To show variations of cardinal vowels, the following diacritics are authorized by the IPA:

ã	nasalized	a̠	retracted
a̟	advanced	ï	centralised ([ï] = [ɨ])
e̩	close	e̜	open
oᵓ	lips more rounded	oᶜ	lips less rounded
a˙	half long	:	long
	ău	weaker element of diphthong	

Further Reading

Jones (1922) provides one of the earliest accounts of cardinal vowel theory, and many other of his publications made use of and described the system (most of these are referenced in Abercrombie (1967) chapter 10). Most British and European texts also have descriptions of the system, though many American publications do not overtly utilize the Cardinal Vowel System, perhaps preferring a classification based on articulatory instrumentation (see Dew and Jensen, 1977). The challenge to the traditional view on vowel description by Wood (1982) is referred to above. References in the Disordered Speech section above cover some of the work on vowels and disordered speech, to which we can add Shriberg and Kent (1982) and Ball (1988a).

CHAPTER 10

Primary, Secondary and Double Articulations

As we have seen, the description of the articulation of a speech sound is generally given in what is called a 'three-term label'. For consonants this consists of voicing, place and manner of articulation; for vowels, lip shape, horizontal and vertical position. However, for any speech sound there are many other aspects of vocal tract activity that *could* be described. Normally, they are not, because usually they are not of major significance in distinguishing one sound from another.

Sometimes, however, it is necessary to describe articulatory aspects of a sound other than the main, or *primary*, stricture. Any other such aspect is termed a *secondary* articulation. It is secondary because it is of less importance than the primary stricture, and also because it is generally a 'weaker' articulation. By this we mean that it will be lower on an articulatory 'strength' scale running from stop as the strongest, through fricative, approximant to vowel or resonant as the weakest.

Sometimes, also, we get sounds where two articulatory strictures are present, yet neither one appears to be more important than the other. This is because both strictures are of the same articulatory strength (e.g. two stops, two fricatives, etc.). In these cases we refer to *double* articulations. In this chapter we will describe both secondary and double articulations.

Secondary articulations

Because of the nature of secondary articulations, involving a weaker constriction than that of the primary, we can really only consider them occurring with consonants (though retroflexion of the tongue tip with vowels is often considered a secondary articulation: see discussion below). In any consonantal articulation we may find a variety of postures adopted by vocal organs (or parts of vocal organs) not involved in producing the primary articulation. For example, in the production of a bilabial consonant (e.g. [b] or [m]) the primary stricture is bilabial. However, although the tongue plays no part in this, it can adopt a variety of positions within the oral cavity. These different positions naturally affect the quality of the speech

56

sound produced, and in some languages these differences can be used to contrast one sound from another (i.e. it can be phonemic). In such cases this secondary articulation obviously needs to be noted in the description of the sound.

Very often, such differences are only an artifact of the phonetic environment, and have no contrastive function. For example, in English the [b] in 'beat' will have a raised, fronted tongue position, while the [b] in 'boot' will have a raised, back tongue position. The reason for this difference lies in the following vowel. The [i] vowel in 'beat' is high, front, while the [u] vowel in 'boot' is high, back. So the secondary articulations here are a result of anticipatory actions of the tongue preparing for the production of the vowels. The sound quality differences between these two [b]s are ignored by English speakers/listeners, and the secondary articulations have no contrastive function, and therefore are generally ignored in descriptions of English phonetics.

While tongue position can vary as a secondary feature during bilabial articulations, so lip position can be a secondary feature during lingual articulations. However, the tongue is a very flexible organ, and we can find both lingual primary and secondary articulations co-occurring (though at different parts of the tongue, naturally).

Phoneticians generally recognize four main types of secondary articulations, named according to their place of occurrence. These are listed below.

1. *Labialization*. A sound is labialized if lip-rounding occurs as a secondary articulation, e.g. [s̹] in English 'soon'; /ʃ/ and /r/ are often labialized in English.

2. *Palatalization*. A sound is palatalized if the tongue is raised to the close front position. Irish has pairs of palatalized and non-palatalized consonants, e.g. /pʲ/ ~ /p/, /tʲ/ ~ /t/.

3. *Velarization*. A sound is velarized if the tongue is raised to the close back position, e.g. [ɫ] or 'dark-l' in English 'fool'.

4. *Pharyngealization*. A sound is pharyngealized if the tongue is lowered and retracted towards the pharynx wall. Arabic has several pairs of pharyngealized (or 'emphatic') and non-pharyngealized consonants, e.g. /tˤ/ ~ /t/, /dˤ/ ~ /d/. The diacritic for pharyngealization is often shown as /t̰/, to distinguish this secondary articulation from velarization, but this is not yet sanctioned by the IPA.

Nasalization has sometimes been considered a secondary articulation, but is more rightly considered a separate phonetic feature of classification (see Chapter 7).

Retroflexion is another feature sometimes considered a secondary articulation. It is true that the curling back of the point of the tongue that occurs in retroflexion can be considered a secondary (or weaker) articulation than the stops, fricatives or approximants with which it can occur. However, as noted in Chapter 6, phoneticians have for long included 'retroflex' as a place of articulation, if only for convenience's sake. Retroflexion with vowels is, however, often still classed as a secondary articulation, as tongue-tip shape is plainly secondary to tongue-body

Figure 10.1 Secondary articulation: [ʈ] ~ [t]

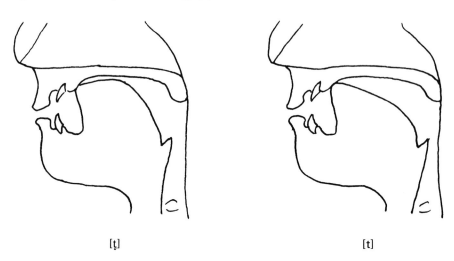

[ʈ]   [t]

shape with vowels. Retroflex (or 'r-coloured') vowels have the point of the tongue curled up and back towards the hard palate. Vowels of this sort occur in many rhotic (r-pronouncing) accents of English, for example in West Country English, or many of the accents of North America in words like 'car' and 'pour'.

Double articulations

As we noted above, a double articulation consists of two simultaneous articulations of equal articulatory strength. These may be two stops (one of which need not be pulmonic egressive), two fricatives or two approximants. Even doubly articulated vowels occur in that lip-rounded vowels can be interpreted as consisting of two equal resonant articulations.

  Where no single IPA symbol exists, double articulations are symbolized with the tie-bar [⁀]. This is somewhat confusing, as this is often used to show affricates (see Chapter 8). Affricates, however, are not double articulations: they are not simultaneous nor are both features of the affricate of equal articulatory weight (this last feature can of course be used to disambiguate the use of the tie-bar in reading transcriptions).

  Double articulations can involve simultaneous labial and lingual strictures, or simultaneous front and back lingual strictures. Examples of double articulations can be seen below.

1. Double stops: [k͡p], [g͡b] as in Igbo; [ŋ͡ɲ] as in Zulu.
2. Double fricatives: [ʃx] as in Swedish (also transcribed as [ɧ]).
3. Double approximants: [ɥ] as in French 'huit'; [w], as in English 'we'.

Figure 10.2 Double articulation: [k͡p]

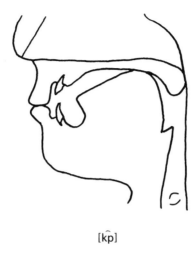

[k͡p]

These double articulations are labelled as follows: [k͡p], 'voiceless labiovelar stop';
[ɥ], 'voiced labiopalatal approximant'; [w], 'voiced labiovelar approximant'.

Disordered speech

Phonological disorders can occur in these areas of speech production as elsewhere.
In such cases normal usages of secondary or double articulations can be abandoned,
or such features can occur where not required. What is more interesting in phonetic
terms are any non-normal secondary or double articulations that occur regularly in
disordered speech. The one area that comes to mind here is that of *sibilance*.
Sibilant sounds often present as a problem area, either due to the lack or to the
excess of the feature. For example, [s] and [z] are often replaced by lateral fricatives
([ɬ] and [ɮ]), which in turn may be reinforced by added sibilance: [ɬ͡ʃ] and [ɮ͡ʒ].
Whereas part of the problem here is in the production of lateral rather than median
fricatives, part is also in the double articulation aimed at adding sibilance.

If channel shape in fricatives (see Chapters 5 and 6) can be considered as a
'secondary' feature of articulation, then the loss of sibilance found with some
speakers might be termed a problem of secondary articulation. These speakers may
replace alveolar grooved fricatives with homorganic slit fricatives (symbolized by
PRDS as [θ̠] and [ð̠].

One final area of consideration with secondary articulations concerns methods
of symbolizing the non-use of these features. Simple non-use requires that the relevant diacritic is not added to the symbol. But in one case only, labialization, can the
actual opposite of the feature occur. In other words, the 'opposite' of palatalization

might be thought of as velarization, whereas the 'opposite' of lip-rounding is not neutral lip-shape, but lip-spreading. If needed to transcribe disordered (or indeed normal) speech, PRDS supply the following symbol: [s̞].

Further reading

Abercombie (1967) provides a description of secondary and double articulations in chapter 4.7, and secondary articulations with vowels are described in Ladefoged (1975, pp. 207f). These features are not covered in detail by other texts which we have referenced. Grunwell (1987) describes many of the patterns of children's articulation problems including some of those mentioned in The Disordered Speech section above.

CHAPTER 11

Suprasegmentals

Up until this chapter we have concentrated on describing segmental aspects of speech: that is to say the individual speech sounds themselves. However, although convenient, this is in several ways an artificial approach. Firstly, it is doubtful whether speech is really divisible into discrete units we can call sounds or 'phones'. The feature of each 'phone' (such as voicing, place, manner, nasality/orality, etc.) do not necessarily have coterminous boundaries, and in reality sounds merge into one another, with different features changing at different points in time. Speech, then, is a dynamic process, not a series of static gestures.

Secondly, there are important aspects of the speech signal that cannot in any way be assigned to segments, however loosely we define that term. There are larger units in speech than the segment, units such as the syllable, the word and the phrase, and there are a range of *suprasegmental* (or prosodic) features which have these units as their domains. The main suprasegmental features we will examine are stress, length and pitch, but we will also examine, later in the chapter, assimilation, another suprasegmental feature and one which demonstrates clearly the non-discrete nature of sound 'segments'.

Stress

The domain of stress is the syllable. The phonetic nature of stress is known: when uttering a stressed syllable the speaker expends more muscular energy. Usually this simply involves more air being pushed out of the lungs through a stronger contraction of the rib-cage muscles. Laryngeal activity may also increase, as may muscular activity in the articulators. All these changes are perceived by listeners as an increase in loudness (see Chapter 14), and often a concomitant raising of pitch (see Chapter 13).

Not all languages use stress in the same way. In some, a particular syllable in every word (e.g. the last, or the next-to-last) is the one which always (or nearly always) receives stress; in others the stress pattern for any word is not predictable, and has to be learnt along with the word itself; in still others, the major stress occurs at the end of a phrase, with other syllables having more or less equal stress. These types can be categorized as follows:

1. fixed word stress: e.g. Czech, Polish, Welsh, Swahili;
2. variable word stress: e.g. English, German, Greek;
3. fixed phrase stress: e.g. French.

Stress patterns contribute to the overall rhythm of a language. Phoneticians' investigations of rhythm have generally focused on how even a rhythm is. Languages where the stressed syllable occurs fairly evenly in terms of the number of syllables between each stressed syllable have been termed 'syllable-timed' (as French), whereas those where the stressed syllables tend to occur at regular intervals of time have been termed 'stress-timed' (as English). The latter are considered less even rhythmically than the former.

In any detailed study of stress, we may need to distinguish primary and secondary (or even more) degrees of stress. This, however, lies in the area of an in-depth investigation of particular languages. In phonetic transcription, stress is marked by ['] before the syllable, e.g. ['ımpɔt] ~ [ım'pɔt], 'import': the noun and the verb respectively. Secondary stress can be shown by [ˌ].

Length

Although length is often expressed in segmental terms, it too has the syllable as its phonetic domain. This is because generally if a syllable has a long vowel it will have a short consonant (or consonants), whereas if the vowel is short the consonant(s) will be longer.

Length differences in vowels appear to be more common than such differences in consonants. Sometimes length is just one of a set of features distinguishing vowels; so, for example, the English [iː] (where [ː] is the diacritic for long) and [ı] vowels as in 'leap' and 'lip' are distinguished by vowel quality (i.e. tongue position) as well as length. A length only distinction is found in English [æː] and [æ], as in 'mad' and 'mat', but this difference is a purely predictable one in English (long before a lenis consonant, short before a fortis one) and not phonemically contrastive.

Some languages, however, can contrast words solely by vowel length. Amongst these are included Korean, Japanese, Arabic, Finnish and Danish. For Estonian it is claimed that there are three degrees of length (with half long being shown by the diacritic [ˑ], which can also be used for any other sub-phonemic difference on vowel length that the phonetician may wish to record).

Examples of vowel length used contrastively can be seen in the following table:

Korean: [il] day	–	[iːl] work
Finnish: [tuleː] comes	–	[tuːleː] blows
Arabic: [qaːla] he said	–	[qaːlaː] they (masc. dual) said
Japanese: [kiro] wear (imp)	–	[kiroː] cut (tentative)

Phonemically contrastive long and short consonants are less usual, but do occur. They are often categorized as double (or geminate) consonants and written with two consonant symbols; in reality, however, the consonant is simply prolonged (in the case of stops, the holding stage is prolonged) for up to twice the length, so this usage is misleading. Examples of 'geminate' consonants can be found in Italian where, for example, ['nonnɔ] means 'grandfather', and ['nonɔ] means 'ninth'. English has some geminates, but these are usually 'accidental' occurrences found at morpheme boundaries: ['bʊk̚keɪs] 'bookcase', [hʌn'nəʊn] 'unknown', ['gaɪlləs] 'guileless'.

Pitch

Pitch changes are controlled mainly through alterations to the tension of the vocal folds. If the folds are stretched, the pitch of the voice will go up (as in a stretched guitar string), and vice versa. Alterations in phonation type (see Chapter 3) may also affect pitch, as, for example, creaky voice will naturally produce a low pitch.

Pitch variations in speech are used in several ways. Firstly, non-linguistic information can be given regarding the speaker's emotions, etc. This obviously lies outside our concerns, as it is extralinguistic information. Secondly, linguistic use can be made of pitch in terms of tone and intonation.

The domain of *tone* is the word. 'Tone languages' are those which have distinctive pitch patterns for individual words either to distinguish lexical meaning or to show grammatical function. A classical example can be found in Standard Chinese, where words can be found with four separate tones:

[ma⁻]	'mother'	high level tone
[ma´]	'hemp'	high rising tone
[ma ˇ]	'horse'	low falling-rising tone
[ma`]	'scold'	high falling tone

Tone languages are found mainly in Africa, the Far East and among American Indian languages.

The domain of *intonation* is the phrase (otherwise known as the word-group, or the tone-group). All languages (including tone languages) have a system of pitch variations linked to the phrase, though there may be considerable differences in how the systems work. Intonation usually has a syntactic function, in that it can break long utterances up into shorter linguistic units, and can be used to distinguish statements from questions or commands. It also has a semantic function, that it can signal in English, for example, that syntactic statements are in fact to be interpreted as questions (''Jane's here?''), to express sarcasm, disbelief, and so on.

We have not the space here to go into detail on the intonation of English, but we can briefly look at the anatomy of intonation. Phoneticians disagree on detail and terminology, but generally accept that each intonation phrase contains one important pitch movement (the tonic or nucleus) with preceding and following patterns of pitch levels. The number of tonics / nuclei, and the number of possible combinations of these with pretonic / prenuclear patterns varies from account to account, but as an example, O'Connor and Arnold (1973) posit seven nuclear tones, and ten emphatic and ten non-emphatic overall intonation groupings. Each of these latter will have its own syntactic and semantic associations. Intonation is obviously an area warranting further study, particularly for the speech pathology student. We return to disordered speech and intonation below.

Assimilation

Some authorities distinguish between 'similitudes' (subphonemic assimilation) and assimilation proper (phonemic assimilation). This distinction is, however, a phonological one, and on the phonetic level both features are basically the same.

The domain of the assimilation can stretch from the boundary between two segments to word boundaries and beyond. The term describes the process whereby one sound becomes more like a neighbouring (though not necessarily an immediately neighbouring) sound. 'More like' might involve just one phonetic feature (e.g. voicing, orality), or more features right up to complete assimilation whereby the two sounds become identical.

Most assimilations are 'compulsory', in that speakers will always use them (though physically it is usually possible to avoid them if one really tries). Juxtapositional assimilation (that is changes across word-boundaries) can sometimes be ignored in formal speaking, though the result may sound stilted.

Some subphonemic assimilations in English can be seen in the following examples:

[k̟] in [k̟ɪt], 'kit' — front 'k' under the influence of the front vowel;

[k̠] in [k̠ɑt], 'cart' — back 'k' under the influence of the back vowel;

[s̹] in [s̹un], 'soon' — rounded 's' influenced by the rounded vowel;

[æ̃] in [mæ̃n], 'man' — nasalized vowel influenced by the nasal stops.

Juxtapositional assimilations are very common in English. These generally affect final alveolars which are influenced by the initial consonant of the following word (this is termed 'regressive' as opposed to 'progressive' assimilation due to the direction of the influence). In English these changes are all phonemic, and examples include:

/t/ → /p/ in /'ðæp 'bɔɪ/, 'that boy';

/t/ → /k/ in /'ðæk 'gɜl/, 'that girl';

/n/ → /m/ in /'wʌm 'pen/, 'one pen';

/n/ → /ŋ/ in /'wʌŋ 'kɪt/, 'one kit';

/s/ → /ʃ/ in /'ðɪʃ 'ʃɒp/, 'this shop'.

Whereas most of this type of assimilation in English involves place of articulation, assimilations in other languages can also involve voicing, and orality/nasality.

Assimilations, then, give us proof that a sound is not a discrete unit: its influence may spread, or rather, different aspects of the sound have their own separate dynamics.

Disordered speech

All the features examined in this chapter may be disordered in the non-normal speaker. With stress we can find non-normal stress placement, reduction of stress, or overextension of stress (in dysarthric and aphasic patients). If necessary, exceptionally heavy stress can be marked with ["].

Another feature associated with stress is the loss of unstressed syllables. While this is developmentally normal (see for example Grunwell, 1987), if it persists it will need to be treated. While it is generally the preceding unstressed syllable which is deleted (e.g. ['nɑnə] < /bə'nɑnə/), sometimes a following one will be affected (e.g. [ʌm'bwel] < /ʌm'brelə/).

In terms of length, we can find excessively short or overlengthened segments. Again, these may occur with dysarthric patients, or also with stutterers. Also we may find periods of silence between segments, syllables or words with these patients. PRDS transcriptions recommended for these are:

1. short: [m̆],[θ̆], [ĭ];
2. prolonged: [m:], [m::];
3. silence: [ʌn-də], [ʌn--də], [ʌn---də] etc.

Again, concerning intonation problems, we do not the space necessary to go into full details. Patients suffering various degrees of hearing loss tend to have difficulties in this area, as naturally will those with certain kinds of laryngeal disorder as well as a range of neurologically caused dysarthrias. Patients presenting with right hemisphere brain damage can also show impairments in prosody, and this is discussed in Code (1987). An adequate transcription of normal speech can usually be adapted to cope with the non-normal. The various diacritic systems used for marking pitch movements can be adapted to describe deaf speech and its atypical intonation patterns; though it should be remembered that other suprasegmental problems occur with these patients, including those to do with tempo and loudness, as well as segmental problems.

Difficulties in producing the coarticulatory effects of assimilation may occur with various categories of patient; however, phonetically the results will not produce any speech events that we have not already discussed.

Finally, a 'suprasegmental' feature of any transcription might well be uncertainty. For technical or other reasons, clinical phoneticians often need to record that a sound, or a whole string of sounds, is to a lesser or greater degree unclear. PRDS suggests the ring is used for this purpose: so O means uncertain segment, ⊙ unspecified consonant, ⊙ unspecified fricative, ⊙ probably [p], etc. The chart in Appendix 2 gives full details on this usage, and on the use of the asterisk and how to show masking by extraneous noise.

Further reading

There are many good descriptions of suprasegmental features that you may wish to consult, including Brosnahan and Malmberg (1970), chapter 7 on coarticulations and chapter 8 on prosodic features, Ladefoged (1975) chapter 10, Wells and Colson (1971) chapters 12 and 21, and Catford (1988) chapter 9. Dew and Jensen (1977) discuss coarticulation in chapter 5, and other prosodic features in chapter 2 and chapter 6.

Introductions to the intonation of English are numerous, and O'Connor and Arnold (1973) and Halliday (1970) are the most commonly used texts for British English, while Trager and Smith (1957) provide a similar account for American English.

Descriptions of disordered intonation are mostly contained in works on deafness and language. A good introduction to this topic is found in Crystal (1980), and more can be found in Wolff (1973).

CHAPTER 12

Instrumentation

When studying articulatory phonetics, the phonetician is able to rely to a great extent on his/her own proprioceptive abilities to work out what the vocal organs were doing at any particular point in time. However, certain areas of the vocal tract are not very suited to such activity (e.g. the larynx), and our own self-reporting may not be too accurate or very detailed. Therefore, phoneticians will use instrumental techniques to confirm their descriptions of articulatory events, and to discover more detail in areas where we are uncertain.

For the speech pathologist and clinical phonetician, instrumental techniques are most important. With disordered speech it may be very difficult to discover precisely what is occurring during speech by non-instrumental means, and these details may be important for an adequate diagnosis and treatment plan. However good are our abilities at impressionistic transcription, there may be relevant features of the speech production process that can only be described via instrumentation. Furthermore, some instrumentation may be designed to play a dual role: investigation and remediation.

Phonetic instrumentation exists for all areas of speech science: articulatory, acoustic and auditory phonetics. In this chapter we will be concentrating on techniques that are primary articulatory, while the other areas will be dealt with in Parts II and III of this book respectively. We will here look at some of the more important experimental techniques that can be used to study different aspects of speech production.

X-radiography

Potentially one of the most helpful of experimental techniques, X-radiography suffers from the drawback of the danger of overexposure. Nevertheless, this method has been utilized in many studies of both normal and disordered speech (see review in Ball, 1984). Still X-ray pictures of course have a limited value in the investigation of the dynamic nature of speech, but X-radiography can be combined with cine, or increasingly nowadays, video to produce valuable evidence. If also combined with fluorography, a technique that uses low dosage radiation, there is justification for its use in experimental procedures. The technique gives us information on a variety of aspects of speech production: articulation (though lateral views are preferred as the bone mass of the jaw makes front views difficult to interpret); larynx position and activity (though vocal fold activity is not easy to measure); and, if necessary, even respiratory activity.

In disordered speech, the technique has most often been used in the study of articulation disorders, and of cleft palate patients (pre- and post-operatively). Other disorders, however, have also been investigated by this method, including stuttering. For a combination of this approach with laryngography, see below.

The main obstacle to regular clinical use of this technique, is the danger of exposure to radiation noted above. This usually means that potential users of X-radiography in speech pathology clinics will need to liaise with the medical authorities responsible for the equipment.

Electromyography

Another technique not restricted to any one point in the speech production process is electromyography (EMG). However, this method is concerned only with the measurement of muscle activity, so can tell us little about the actual positioning of the vocal organs in speech. It operates by recording via electrodes the electrical activity that occurs during the firing of the motor units of the muscles (see Moore, 1984, for a full description and review of studies). These signals are then processed, and can be presented in readable form via a chart (or ink-jet) recorder. By analyzing the resultant print-out we can see which muscles 'fired' at which point in time during speech. This is not only important for the study of normal speech, but also, of course, for the investigation of various speech disorders. Particularly stuttering, but also other disorders where speech organ coordination is especially important, have benefitted from EMG studies (e.g. dysarthria and apraxia of speech).

The limitations on EMG revolve around the positioning of the electrodes. Surface electrodes are suitable for the investigation of, for example, the orbicularis oris muscle (involved with lip-rounding), but for others needle electrodes may be needed. These are naturally uncomfortable, and there is a limit to where such electrodes can be conveniently placed. However, Catford (1977) notes that EMG can be used with up to sixty or seventy muscles, these being the most important ones in speech.

Aerometry

Aerometry is a technique designed to examine air flow through the vocal tract. It does this through the use of a face mask within which both ingressive and egressive

Figure 12.1 Aerometry trace of (a) a normal and (b) a hypernasal speaker saying 'eighteen, nineteen, twenty'

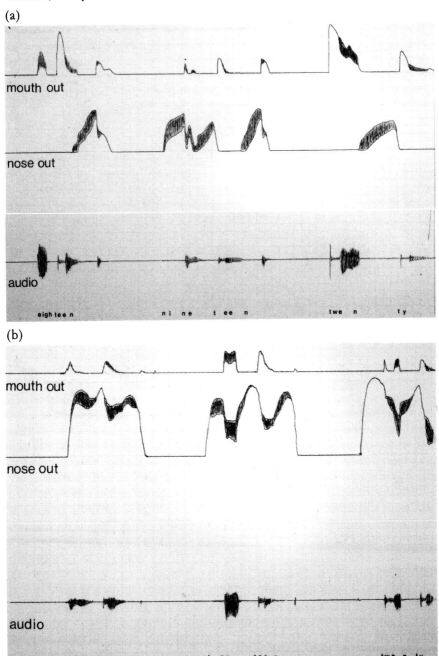

air flow is measured, through both the oral and nasal cavities. The mask will also usually contain a microphone, so that the resultant traces via a chart recorder can easily be compared with a trace of the acoustic signal. For a full description and review of studies, see Anthony and Hewlett (1984).

This technique can examine aspects of initiation (for example, amounts of air flow with different air stream mechanisms), orality and nasality, and even articulation (for example, comparing aspirated, fortis plosives with unaspirated, lenis ones). In clinical phonetics, the greatest use of this technique has been with cleft palate patients, or those with other velopharyngeal inadequacy. We are able to learn how much difference, if any, there exists with these patients between target nasal and target oral sounds.

Various other devices for measuring different aspects of air flow are described in Catford (1977, pp. 239f), but aerometry is the only one used with any regularity in clinical studies. Figure 12.1 shows a comparison between aerometry traces of normal and disordered speakers.

Laryngography

This technique (sometimes termed *glottography*, or more properly *electrolaryngography*) is one of several methods of investigating larynx activity. The particular aspect of this activity that is measured is vocal fold vibration. It operates through the use of two surface electrodes, placed externally on either side of the larynx. A weak current is passed from one electrode to the other through the larynx, and the equipment is able to measure the varying impedance offered to this current by the vibrating vocal folds, and thus give information of glottal behaviour. The resultant data is often displayed on oscilloscope screens, but can be converted to 'hard-copy' via a chart recorder.

The electrolaryngograph not only gives us information as to voiced/voiceless states of phonation (as well as other types of course), but it can also display information as to the pitch of the voice (derived of course from the changes in frequency of vocal fold vibration). In clinical work the electrolaryngograph is most often used in the study and remediation of intonational problems (see Chapter 11). In terms of remediation, the device allows a clinician to show a target pitch pattern that a patient can aim to reproduce.

Coupled with a particular form of X-radiography known as xero-radiography, electrolaryngography has been used to investigate voice disorders (see Chapter 3). This combined technique, known as XEL, is described in Ball (1984), and in Abberton and Fourcin (1984) who also describe the principles of electrolaryngography in detail, together with a review of studies using this technique.

Palatography

As its name suggests, this technique is concerned with measuring vocal activity concerning the roof of the mouth. In this, it is only of use in the investigation of articulation and articulation disorders. The technique takes varying forms, but most in use today is electropalatography (see Hardcastle, *et al.*, 1989, for a review). In this method use is made of an artificial palate, accurately shaped to the subject's mouth. This has on it a number of electrodes which record the position of any contact between the tongue and palate. Through this method we can get an accurate picture from the resultant palatograms of the different articulations of normal speech, with which we can compare palatograms from patients suffering from a variety of articulation disorders. Figure 12.2 shows palatograms of normal and disordered speech.

Figure 12.2 Single palatogram frames selected at a point of maximum stable contact during production of /s/ in the word 'sun': (a) a normal speaker, [sʌn]; (b) a child with a lateral /s/, [ɬʌn]; (c) a child with a cleft palate, [çʌn]

ROW

NUMBER

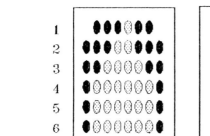
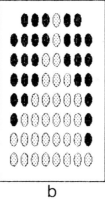
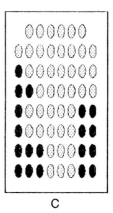

Further reading

Keller (1971) is one of the few books devoted entirely to instrumental techniques in articulatory phonetics, and covers most of the procedures described in this chapter. Code and Ball (1984) is devoted to descriptions of many techniques (some of them articulatory) of use to speech pathologists and clinical linguistics. Hardcastle *et al.*, (1989) is an up-to-date account of electropalatography, while Abberton *et al.* (1989) provides a survey of electrolaryngography.

PART II
Acoustic Phonetics

CHAPTER 13

Frequency and Pitch

In Part I of this book we looked at the physical actions necessary to produce speech. The end result of these is the production of *sound waves* which are transmitted to the listener(s). The study of these sound waves is called *acoustic phonetics*.

Sound waves are disturbances in the molecules of air, and they travel in a way described below. For speech, of course, these disturbances originate in the production of an air flow, and the modifications of this air flow by phonation, articulation and so on. Speech communication, then, can be seen as a process whereby linguistic 'units' in the brain are converted to neural commands, then to muscle activity and finally to sound waves. At the other end of the speech chain (see Part III) these sound waves are converted back to physical movement, neural commands and then mental images in the listener's brain.

Sound waves

To get an understanding of how sound 'works', we can take the example of a simple sound producer: a guitar string. If the string is plucked, it will move away from its position of rest position (1) in Figure 13.1 below to a new position (2). Dependent on the force used to pluck the string, (2) will be a greater or less distance away from (1). However, a fixed object, when moved, will always try to return to its rest position, so having reached (2), the string will move back towards (1). As it moves, it builds up a momentum, and so overshoots (1), and reaches a position (3), about as far to the other side of (1) as (2) was in the first direction. As we can see in Figure 13.2, this motion is of a wave-form, and the guitar string will continue this wave, until the motion decreases (or is 'damped') by the gradual absorption of energy by the string and the guitar itself.

Now, if we consider what happened to air in the vicinity of the guitar string, we can see that the wave motion of the string sets up a wave motion of air. The movements of the string set up alternate high and low air pressures, affecting particles (or

Figure 13.1 The movement of a guitar string

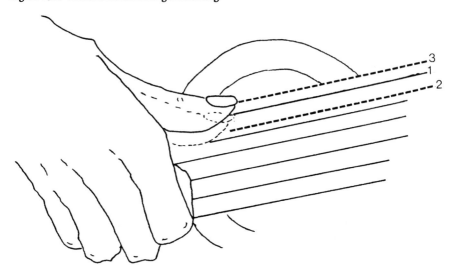

Figure 13.2 A simple sine wave

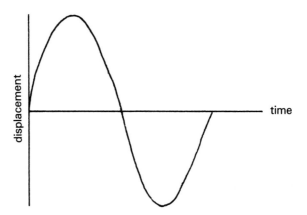

molecules) of air in different ways. The pressure changes 'ripple' through the air in a way similar to the ripples on a pond which spread out from wherever a stone has been thrown in. Of course, these sound waves do not continue for ever. The length of time the sound continues before dying out depends to some extent on the amount of energy expended in setting the wave in motion initially. But most importantly, it depends on the resistance of the physical forces that oppose the vibratory motion that causes the sound. These include the surrounding air, the metal in a tuning fork (for example), the body of a guitar, etc. Some things damp down sound waves faster than others, and indeed in acoustics we refer to this as the property of 'damping'.

A wave-form such as in Figure 13.2 is known as a simple sine wave, but in speech there is not a simple, single source of the sound waves such as there is in a tuning fork. The various components of the vocal tract all add their own characteristics to the air flow (see Chapter 15), such that we are left with a complex wave-form: i.e., a wave-form made up of several simple wave-forms (see below for discussion of periodic and aperiodic waves). An example of a complex wave-form is given in Figure 13.3, and it shows the wave-form used in pronouncing the vowel [ɔ], of 'caught'.

Figure 13.3 The complex wave of [ɔ]

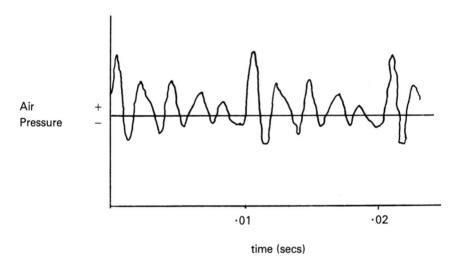

Air Pressure +/−

·01   ·02

time (secs)

There are various ways to observe the wave-forms of sounds, and perhaps the most useful of these is an oscillograph attached to a chart recorder. Oscillomink devices can record not only the wave-form, but pitch and intensity as well if combined with the correct instruments. However, they are not able to give full details of the wave form, as they are constrained by the speed with which the ink-jets can themselves move. A more useful instrument for investigating acoustic phonetics is the sound spectrograph, discussed in Chapter 17.

Frequency

Frequency is an important aspect of sound waves, and one that we will need to study in relation to speech sounds. Let us return to our guitar string. We saw in Figures 13.1 and 13.2 that by plucking the string we create a wave movement and thereby a sound wave. The movement of the string (or, of course, the air particle) from position (1) to (2) and then to (3) and back again to (1) is called a *cycle*. To find out the frequency of this sound, we need to know how many cycles will be completed in a given time, i.e. how frequent is the movement from starting position through the displacement positions and back to starting position.

In acoustics the period of time we take for measuring purposes is one second: so frequency is expressed in cycles per second, more commonly called Hertz (Hz). Therefore, if we say a sound wave has a frequency of 100Hz, we mean that in one second there will be 100 complete cycles, or in other words a cycle is completed every 10 msec (milliseconds). Figure 13.4 shows simple sine waves of varying frequencies.

Figure 13.4 Sine waves of different frequencies

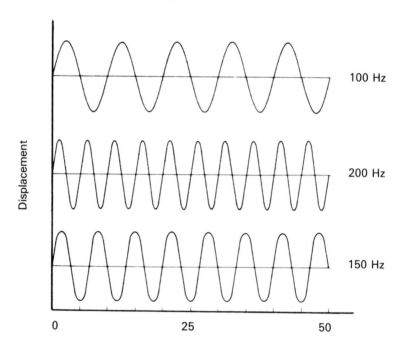

As noted earlier, the sounds of speech are not simple waves of the type shown in Figure 13.4, but complex wave-forms, often built up from a series of simple forms. Even so, the frequency of the various component parts of these sounds can be measured and used to classify these sounds. While many speech sounds are *periodic* (in that, however complex, the patterns reoccur in the same way), others (such as voiceless fricatives) are *aperiodic* (in that the sound shows no discernible repeated aspects). A contrast between these two types is shown in Figure 13.5.

Figure 13.5 Periodic and aperiodic sounds

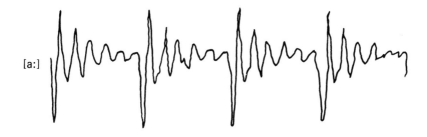

[a:]

[s]

Any complex periodic wave-form has a *fundamental frequency*. In fact, our guitar string will have a complex wave-form, and we have only been investigating the fundamental frequency so far (see Fry, 1979, for more details of this concept). The other frequencies that occur above the fundamental frequency are termed *harmonics*, and are multiplications of that fundamental. For example, a fundamental frequency of 100 Hz, will have a second harmonic at 200 Hz, a third at 300 Hz and so on. If the fundamental frequency were 160Hz, the second harmonic would be 320Hz, the third 480Hz, etc. In speech, the fundamental frequency is provided by vocal fold vibration (which is why voiceless sounds are aperiodic in that they lack this feature) with a harmonic series based on that rate, which is constantly changing in speech. We will return to the acoustic make-up of individual sounds in later chapters, but will turn our attention next to the main role of the fundamental frequency in speech: pitch.

Pitch

We have already examined the articulatory nature of pitch (see Chapter 11) and its linguistic use in intonation and tone. Acoustically we have to ensure we remember that, although related, frequency and pitch are not the same. While frequency is a physical property of sound waves, pitch is the auditory realization (i.e. impression) of that property. In other words, we *hear* pitch.

As we noted above, pitch is derived from the fundamental frequency of vocal fold vibration, which is continuously changing through speech. The average fundamental frequencies in speech are 120Hz for males, 225Hz for females, and 265Hz for children. The total range of fundamental frequencies found in speech extends from 60Hz to 500Hz (figures from Fry, 1979, p. 68).

While frequencies are measured in Hz, perceived pitch is measured in Mels, which is a scale of perceptual values. This scale is logarithmic, in that it increases not by regular amounts, but by multiplication of units. This reflects the fact that we perceive high and low pitch in this way. For example, the ear is more sensitive to pitch changes in lower frequencies than in higher, and the Mel scale reflects this. Ladefoged (1962) gives examples of Mel measurements as compared to frequencies in Hz (Table 13.1). The Mel scale (see Figure 24.5) is derived from psychophysical experimentation, and is therefore not a purely objective measurement system. An alternative method of describing pitch (the Koenig scale) is illustrated in Ladefoged (1962, p. 77), but this also is a perceptual scale.

Table 13.1   Mel measurements compared to Hertz frequencies

Pitch in Mels	Frequency in Hz
0	20
250	160
500	394
750	670
1000	1000
1250	1420
1500	1900
1750	2450
2000	3120
2250	4000

Suprasegmental aspects of disordered speech were briefly discussed in Chapter 11, and we also saw in Chapter 12 how the electrolaryngograph can be used to examine the fundamental frequency produced by vocal fold vibration. The acoustic manifestation of this activity can be examined via, for example, speech spectrography which is discussed below (see Chapters 17 and 21 in particular).

Disorders in pitch production also have ramifications in perceptual phonetics, and this area is returned to in Chapter 24 in Part 3 of this book. The ultimate 'disorder' in this respect is the loss of the larynx in laryngectomy, thus removing the natural source of pitch production.

Further reading

One of the best introductions to acoustic aspects of speech is Fry (1979), though a briefer account can be found in Ladefoged (1962). Standard phonetic texts often cover the field as well, and good accounts can be found in Brosnahan and Malmberg (1970) chapter 2, and Ladefoged (1975) chapter 8. More advanced texts also exist, of course, the two best known of these, perhaps, being Lehiste (1967) and Fry (1976). These are collections of papers, some of which will be of use to supplement other chapters in this part of the book.

CHAPTER 14

Intensity and Loudness

Amplitude

In the previous chapter we looked at the frequency of sound waves, i.e. the number of times per second that the pattern of the wave is repeated. Another important aspect of the sound wave concerns the characteristics of the cycle itself. The amplitude of a sound wave is the amount of variation in the air pressure from normal that is occasioned by the sound making device. To return to our example of the guitar string: if this is plucked with great force, it will move further away from its rest position than if it is plucked with lesser force (see Figure 14.1, a and b). The sound waves resulting from such actions will also differ in a similar way, in terms of greater or less disturbance of the air pressure. Amplitude, then, is directly dependent upon physical actions. Figure 14.2 illustrates the sound waves of identical frequencies, but with different amplitudes. To measure amplitude one would need to use the system employed for measuring changes in air pressure: the barometric scale. However, for speech purposes, it is much more common to measure differences in intensity, rather than amplitude.

Intensity

In the same way that we perceive differences of frequency as pitch changes, so we perceive intensity as loudness. But what exactly is intensity? If we increase the amplitude of a sound it appears louder: for example if we displace our guitar string more than usual (i.e. pluck it harder!) then we get a louder note. However, amplitude is independent of frequency, in that we can have sound waves of the same amplitude but different frequencies (as well as of the same frequency but different amplitudes as in Figure 14.2 above). It may be easily understood, perhaps, that in the example of two waves with identical amplitudes but where the first has a lower frequency than the second, the second sound wave uses more energy, for it needs to complete its cycle more often than the first. Indeed, this second sound wave will be

Figure 14.1 A guitar string plucked with differing force

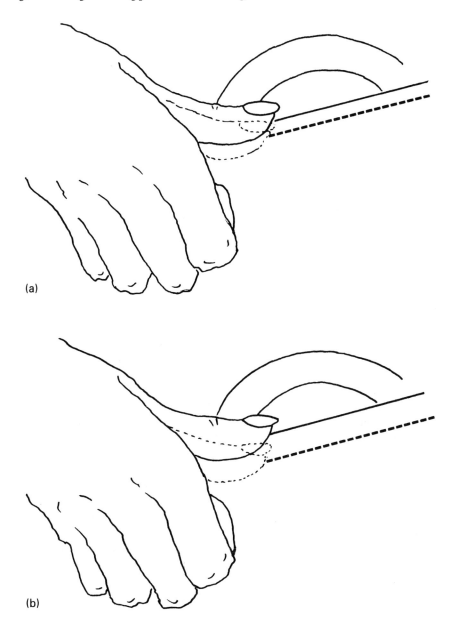

(a)

(b)

Figure 14.2 Waves of different amplitude but the same frequency

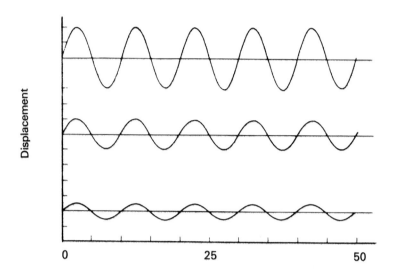

perceived as being louder than the first, despite the fact that their amplitudes are the same.

It appears, then, that loudness is derived not from amplitudes or from frequency separately, but from what we might call the energy input into a sound: a combination of both the amplitude and the frequency. The term given in acoustics to this combination is intensity.

The relationship between the components of intensity (i.e. amplitude and frequency) is a somewhat complicated one. This is because intensity is in a proportional relationship to its components: to the square of the frequency and the square of the amplitude. Fry (1979) gives examples of how this works: if we double the amplitude of a 100 Hz sound, we increase the intensity by four; if we treble it we increase the intensity by nine. Similarly, if we keep the amplitude static, but compare sounds of different frequencies, we find that a 200 Hz sound has four times the intensity of a 100 Hz sound, and a 400 Hz sound will have sixteen times the intensity of the 100 Hz sound. Of course, combinations of frequency and amplitude differences will result in changes of intensity involving the sum of both squares. As we noted in Chapter 13, speech sounds are all complex sound waves, where the working out of individual frequencies and amplitudes is difficult. Therefore, the concept of intensity is a useful single comparison measure.

Loudness

Loudness is, as we have noted, the perceptual correlate to intensity, and in acoustic phonetics we are often interested in how much louder one sound (or indeed one speaker) is compared to another. The important point here are the words 'compared to'. Rather than an absolute measure of intensity/loudness, we are more interested in a relational measurement. This measurement system is the decibel (dB) scale. A full description of the decibel scale is provided in Fry (1979), but for our purposes here we may note that the scale is both ratio-based and logarithmic. Ladefoged (1962) states: 'The difference in decibels between two sounds is defined as ten times the common logarithm of their power ratios' (p. 82). To clarify this statement we can repeat Ladefoged's explanatory table (Table 14.1).

Table 14.1 Differences in Decibels

Power ratio between sounds	Common log. of power ratio	Difference in decibels
10 to 1	1	10
100 to 1	2	20
1000 to 1	3	30

Source: Ladefoged (1962, p.82).

It is important to stress here that these dB values do not belong to an absolute scale, but express a difference between two previously noted sounds. However, we are all aware of the use of the scale in common parlance as if it *were* an absolute one. This is because it is commonly used in comparison to a standard intensity: the threshold of hearing (10^{-16} watts of energy, or the sound pressure of 0.0002 dynes/cm^2). Fry (1979, p. 93) notes that when a sound is described simply as 90 dB, it has an intensity of 90 dB higher than 10^{-16} watts, and the ratio of intensities is one thousand million to one.

Table 14.2 Decibel Scale of Common Sound Intensities

Intensity (dB)	Sound
130	four-engined jet plane, 120 ft
120	threshold of pain; pneumatic hammer, 3 ft
110	boilermaker's shop; rock band
100	car horn, 15 ft; symphony orchestra *fortissimo*
90	pneumatic drill, 4 ft; lorry, 15 ft
80	noisy underground train; loud radio music
75	telephone bell, 10 ft
70	very busy city traffic, 70 ft
60	conversation, 3 ft; car 30 ft
50	quiet office
40	residential area no traffic; quiet conversation
30	quiet garden; whispered conversation
20	watch ticking at ear; broadcast studio
10	rustle of leaves
0	threshold of audibility

In giving dB measurements in this way it is important to note the distance from the source that the measurement takes place. This is becasue as we increase our distance from the sound source the intensity falls off. Table 14.2 (adapted from Fry, 1979, p.94) notes the distance from source of the sound types, something that is often omitted in non-technical descriptions.

Intensity and speech

We can see from Table 14.2 that 60 dB is the sound level of normal conversation at a distance of 3 ft. This, of course, is an average figure. Speakers vary in the loudness of their voices, and naturally their speech will become louder or softer dependent upon circumstances. Furthermore, within speech certain sounds have greater intensity than others. This fact has already been discussed in Chapter 4 when describing syllable theory, and will be referred to again in Part III of this book (Chapter 24). Table 14.3 (adapted from Fry, 1979, p.127) gives the relative intensity of English vowels and consonants with reference to the intensity of [θ] which, being the English sound with the least intensity, was assigned no value.

Table 14.3 Relative Intensity of English Sounds based on [θ]

Vowel	Intensity		Vowel	Intensity
ɔ	29		m	17
ɒ	28		tʃ	16
ɑ	26		n	15
ʌ	26		d	13
ɜ	25		ʒ	13
æ	24		z	12
ʊ	24		s	12
e	23		t	11
ɪ	22		g	11
u	22		k	11
i	22		v	10
w	21		ð	10
r	20		b	8
j	20		d	8
l	20		p	7
ʃ	19		f	7
ŋ	18		θ	0

The intensity of sounds in human speech is measured mainly through the analysis of sound spectrograms, a technique described in Chapter 17.

Intensity and disordered speech

In disordered speech a failure to control intensity is perhaps most often noted at the prosodic level, i.e. an inappropriate use of loudness across an entire utterance (this may, of course, be an utterance produced too loudly or not loudly enough). It is also possible that the intensity ratio between individual sounds (as in Table 14.3) may be disturbed, leading to distortion and a confusion between sounds on the part of the listener.

Failure to control for overall loudness is a disorder most commonly associated with the deaf. It is clear that the main feedback control that normal speakers use for loudness is aural, and a loss of this feedback system often leads to fluctuations between extremes of intensity. This can easily be tested by the temporary removal of aural feedback in normal speakers (through the use of earphones, etc.), and a note being made of resultant disturbances in the loudness of the subject's utterances.

In dysarthria caused by Parkinson's disease, the disruption to loudness often results in inaudible speech.

Further reading

The texts referred to at the end of the previous chapter can also be used to supplement reading on this topic. The topic of aural feedback is returned to in Chapter 30.

CHAPTER 15

Resonance

We have looked so far at two important areas of acoustics: frequency and intensity. We have seen that frequency (perceived as pitch) refers to the number of times the sound wave completes its cycle in a second, and that intensity (perceived as loudness) refers to the amount of acoustic energy involved in the production of the sound wave. As far as speech is concerned, both these features are eventually derived from the source of sound in the vocal tract, (usually) a pulmonic egressive air stream modified by the laryngeal voice-source. However, we know that individual speech segments sound different. Further, we know that individual speakers sound different. In this chapter we will be looking at what causes these differences.

Free vibrations and forced vibrations

The example we have been using in the previous chapters of the sound wave produced by plucking a guitar string is termed in acoustics a 'free vibration'. This implies that the sound is produced through the application of a force (in our case the plucking motion of the finger) which is then removed. Free vibrations may result in simple sound waves (such as those produced from tuning forks), or complex waves (for example our guitar string) having a fundamental frequency and a range of harmonics (see Chapter 13).

However, there is another way in which sound can be produced: what is termed 'forced vibration'. Unlike free vibration, where the force that starts the vibration is removed, with forced vibration that force is constantly applied. This results in a system (the 'driven system') that is being 'forced' to vibrate by being brought into contact with a 'driving force' (usually an already vibrating system).

The usual example employed to demonstrate this difference is the tuning fork. If we strike a tuning fork (let us assume the usual musical type, tuned to A) we hear a pure tone of 440 Hz frequency. However, this sound is not great, and can only be heard if we position the fork near the ear. To make the sound louder is a straightforward matter, however; we can simply press the foot of the fork onto a table top or desk top. By pressing the fork onto the table we are driving the table top with the vibrations of the fork: we are in effect setting up a forced vibration. The table then is emitting a sound wave 'caused' by the tuning fork. Its frequency will be that of the driving force, i.e. 440 Hz for an A fork, or 264 Hz for a C fork, and so on. Note that in these instances the table is responding to the driving force; the frequencies emitted are not that of the table itself. If we strike the table top to produce free vibration, we find that the resultant sound dies away swiftly, and is completely unlike what happens with our tuning fork experiment.

The principle of forced vibrations is utilized in many musical intruments. Our guitar string does not by itself cause sound waves of great intensity when plucked, but (in acoustic guitars at least) the vibrations of the string are the driving force which drives the body of the guitar, and this results in much louder sounds. Solid-body electric guitars do not rely on this process, and if a string is plucked when the guitar is not turned on, you will hear how quiet the sound of the string alone is.

Resonance

Resonance is the term used to describe the phenomenon of one system being set in motion by the vibrations of another: one system 'resonates' the other. However, the end result of this action depends upon the acoustic properties of the driving force and of the driven system. The loudness of the forced vibration depends on two main factors. Firstly we need to consider how closely coupled the driving force and the driven system are. With the tuning fork and the table top we will get a louder forced vibration when the fork is pressed against the table then if it is held just slightly above it. Even in the latter case, however, the vibrations will pass through the air to the table.

Perhaps more importantly, however, is the relation between the natural frequencies of the two systems. We will get the greatest amplitude of the forced vibrations when the natural frequency[1] of the driving force is the same as the natural frequency of the driven system. In this condition, the two systems are in sympathy, though when the frequencies are near one another, even if not identical, we still find a greater amplitude in the forced vibrations than when they differ considerably. This aspect of resonance can be seen in a 'resonance curve', as in Figure 15.1 below. (As discussed in Chapter 13, 'damping' is the absorption of energy to overcome the force of friction in a vibrating system. The amount of damping that occurs depends on the physical properties of the system concerned.) Figure 15.1 shows that a lightly damped system produces forced vibrations of great amplitude, but only near the point of resonance: that is where the frequencies of the two systems are in sympathy. On the other hand, although a highly damped system produces lesser amplitude, this is spread out over a great range of frequencies. The former type is often described as 'sharply tuned'.

Phonetics for Speech Pathology

Figure 15.1 Resonance curves for lightly damped and highly damped systems

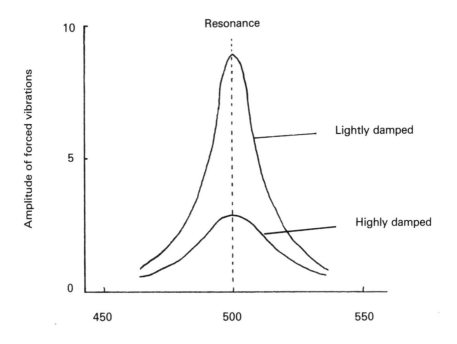

Frequency of driving force (Hz)

Resonance and complex waves

We have seen how forced vibrations are most effective when the natural frequencies of the two systems coincide. But what happens when the driving force, as in speech, is not a simple tone of one natural frequency but a complex tone having more than one frequency and associated harmonics? The answer is straightforward: as long as the natural frequency of the driven system is included in the complex tone of the driver, this frequency will be selected by the resonator and amplified. (Obviously, if it is not included, then the nearest frequency will be amplified to a lesser extent, as seen in Figure 15.1.)

In many instances, such as the vocal tract in speech, or a wind instrument in music, the resonator is adjustable. This means that it can be altered just so that particular frequencies in the driving force can be maximally amplified by the resonator.

Another important property of resonators is that many have different modes of vibration. These are related to different wavelengths, which means that a complex tone in the driving force may well result in resonance in the driven system at a series

Figure 15.2 Multiple resonances

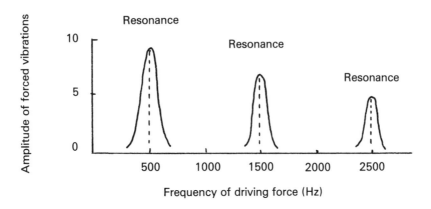

of different wavelengths (or frequencies), though the amplitude of the forced vibrations decreases with the higher frequencies. This is illustrated in Figure 15.2. This is particularly important in speech, where the normal noise source is a complex tone, rich in harmonics (see formants in the following section). The fact that a resonator amplifies certain frequencies also means that it 'ignores' (or 'absorbs') others, as it were. In this respect resonators act as filters, reducing the amplitude of ranges of frequencies. This again is an important feature of the acoustics of speech production.

Sound spectra

This work on resonance allows us a method of classifying speech sounds acoustically. We can do this by examining the *spectra* of the sounds, that is a 'statement of what frequencies are to be found in the mixture and what their relative amplitudes are' (Fry, 1979, p.58). Acoustic analysis of this sort is normally done via speech spectrography (see Chapter 17), but the results can be set out diagrammatically as in Figure 15.3. It is seen that in speech sounds, although the fundamental frequency of speech alters from moment to moment (to create differences in pitch, for example, see Chapter 13), the overall shape (or 'envelope') of each sound is more or less constant.

Figure 15.3 also shows three of the 'resonances' of the vocal tract (see previous section) for the sounds concerned. In speech acoustics we refer to these peaks of amplitude as *formants*. As the vocal tract can alter shape as described in Part I of this book, these formants will occur at different frequencies for different sounds. The identification of formant structure is one important part of the acoustic analysis of voiced speech sounds, and will be returned to in later chapters in this part.

Figure 15.3 Spectra of two speech sounds: [i] and [ɑ]

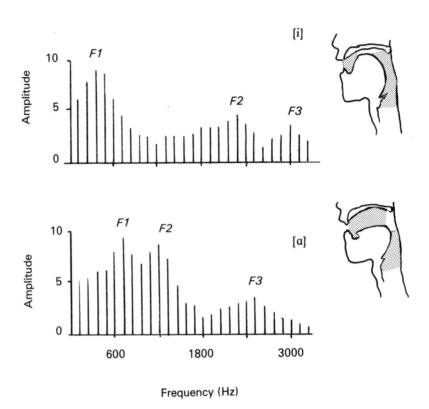

Frequency (Hz)

Disordered speech

In terms of resonance, the main area of interest in disordered speech is the mal-function of parts of the vocal tract — the resonator of speech. (Laryngectomy was referred to in Chapter 13, and will not be returned to here.) The most common resonator problems in speech are concerned with the additions or otherwise of the nasal cavity to the vocal tract resonance system. If physical control of this cavity via the velopharyngeal valve is impaired (through cleft palate or neurological disorder, for instance), then nasal resonance may be present when not required, or absent when required. Hyper- and hyponasality (or as some phoneticians prefer, over- and undernasality) is also discussed in Chapter 7.

Further reading

The topics of this chapter are quite difficult to grasp, and perhaps the best source of further reading is Fry (1979) chapter 5. Ladefoged (1962) also provides a good account of the area in his chapter 5. The topic of hypernasality and velopharyngeal inadequacy was referred to in more detail in Chapter 7.

Note

1. A natural frequency is that which would occur were the system subject to free vibrations.

CHAPTER 16

Recording Speech

Speech, unlike writing, is evanescent; in other words it lacks permanence. If we wish to study the characteristics of speech, therefore, (whether normal or disordered) we must have a way of overcoming this basic characteristic. In Part I of this book we have introduced many of the written symbols phoneticians use when attempting to represent speech on paper, and so to give it a form of permanence and make it easier for us to examine.

However, reducing speech to writing (as the verb 'reduce' suggests) is inevitably a compromise. A transcription which includes the maximum of information obtainable on segmental and suprasegmental aspects of the speech signal is likely to be so 'narrow' (i.e. cluttered) as to make it very difficult to read. Moreover, it will still not give all the information that one can obtain, e.g. the use of the length diacritics ([ˑ] half-long, [ː] long) does not indicate how long in milliseconds a segment actually is. Therefore, phoneticians started to look at other ways of 'capturing' the speech signal to get a permanent record that could then be subject to analysis. Various instrumental techniques were developed (see Chapters 12 and 17) that examined articulatory and acoustic aspects of speech. Perhaps one can say, though, that in recent times the instrumental analysis of speech acoustics has been the most popular.

One of the most frequently used acoustic analysis techniques is speech spectrography, and this is described in more detail in Chapter 17. The spectrograph in its various forms can take direct input of the speech signal, but both this instrument and others used in speech analysis (e.g. the laryngograph) can also use prerecorded speech. Today, the recording of speech is generally done via different types of tape recorder, and in this chapter we will look at how tape recorders work, and how to ensure a good recording for speech analysis purposes, though in recent times computerised speech recording has become more popular.

Tape recorder

We can consider the tape recorder as having three sections: the recording system in terms of the electronics which deal with the input of a sound signal; the mechanical system, which includes the tape which is, of course, the storage part of the instrument; and the replay system, or the electronics responsible for the output of the sound signal from the storage medium.

When considering the suitability of any tape recorder for work with speech, these three parts must be examined. As Tatham (1984) has pointed out, generally speaking the electronic systems of tape recorders are perfectly adequate to dealing with the input and output of acoustic signals. What limits the usefulness of any particular recorder is its mechanical system, including the storage medium: the tape itself. The possible limitations concern the process of getting the signal onto the tape and then keeping it stored there. In these respects we can look at three factors in particular: signal-to-noise ratio, frequency response, and distortion. These factors involve the concepts of frequency and amplitude, introduced in Chapters 13 and 14 respectively.

The signal-to-noise ratio concerns amplitude, and is therefore measured in dB. It describes the range of amplitudes that can be recorded by the machine in question without producing distortion. The dynamic range of speech is generally within 50 dB (i.e. the speech signal of a particular speaker at its greatest amplitude is rarely 50 dB greater than at its lowest amplitude). For speech recording, then, we must ensure the equipment is capable of recording this range, i.e. has a signal-to-noise ratio of 50 dB.

The second factor, frequency response, does not refer simply to the range of frequencies that the recorder can deal with; rather to the range of frequencies that can be recorded without distortion of amplitude. So a statement on frequency response should show not only the range of frequencies (e.g. 45 Hz to 18 kHz), but also the accuracy of amplitude preservation in that range (e.g. ± 2 dB, meaning that fluctuations in amplitude on playback are restricted to 2 dB greater or less).

However, this information may not give us all we need to know about the suitability of equipment for work with speech. We need also to know what the range of amplitudes is within which we can expect this frequency response. A cassette tape recorder can only maintain its frequency response at comparatively low amplitudes, otherwise its frequency response will be considerably reduced. With most cassette machines this limitation is important for speech analysis, for they may well play back high frequencies at reduced amplitudes, whereas open-reel recorders of good quality do not have this problem, maintaining their frequency response at amplitudes high enough for the range of speech in normal circumstances. To guarantee that even an open-reel recorder operates at its best signal-to-noise ratio and frequency response it is essential to use the widest possible tape and the fastest possible tape speed. This provides the maximum possible area of tape on which the signal can be recorded, thereby reducing the possibility of distortion.

Distortion is the last of the three factors mentioned above. It can be caused in a variety of ways including such things as badly maintained equipment or old and damaged tape. Apart from these causes, distortion comes from trying to record an amplitude greater than the maximum allowed for in a piece of equipment. This can be avoided by ensuring that the input signal (the speech signal) does not exceed this maximum, and this can be checked for via the recording meters.

There are several variations of the basic direct tape recording instrumentation that need not detain us here long, and are explained in some detail in Tatham (1984). The most important to note are FM recordings: particularly useful for low frequencies of less than 35 Hz, and proprietary noise reduction systems such as Dolby™, which should definitely not be used in speech analysis.

There are also more recent recording systems which have moved away from the traditional analog method of recording sound to a digital approach. These systems still use tape (although solid state recorders are also becoming available) but undertake the storage in a different way. Again, Tatham (1984) gives full details, but for our purpose we need only be aware that such systems are more than adequate for speech purposes in terms of both signal-to-noise ratio and frequency response.

Recording speech

Within the clinical situation there may be two main purposes in making a speech recording. Firstly we may wish to make a permanent record of a patient's speech from which we will later undertake an impressionistic transcription. On the other hand, we may make the recording in order to provide input to a piece of instrumentation (e.g. a spectrograph) to undertake an acoustic analysis. For both purposes we need to ensure not only that the equipment is suitable, but that the recording is made in the most suitable way. Factors that can influence this include the place where the recording is made, the microphones used, and the settings on the recorder itself.

Location is important in ensuring a good recording, for if an unsuitable location is used, echo may be recorded as well as the main signal. This obviously results in a recording totally unusable for acoustic analysis and unclear for impressionistic transcription. Echo from a non-sound-proofed room is related to the phenomenon of resonance and damping discussed in Chapter 15, and can only be completely avoided if a sound-proof recording studio is available. In the clinical situation this is often impractical; nevertheless, the worst effects of echo can be mitigated by ensuring that a room with curtains, carpets and upholstered furniture is utilized, as this will help absorb the sound. In making a recording it is also important to ensure that unwanted sounds from outside the room are not picked up.

Another important aspect of recording technique lies in the choice of microphone. Two main types of microphone are available: omnidirectional and unidirectional. The omnidirectional type is not suitable for speech work as they will pick up extraneous, unwanted sounds, whereas the unidirectional type can be aimed at the speaker concerned. If we are recording two speakers, two microphones can be used, feeding into different channels of a stereo tape recorder. This will make the interpretation of the playback easier, as we will be able to identify each speaker by concentrating on the different channels. Multitrack machines, though expensive, provide the same ability for larger numbers of speakers. Tatham (1984) gives further information on microphones, and points out that lapel-mounted battery microphones are ideal for clinical speech work.

The final point we need to consider is operating the settings on the machine itself. The most important of these is the gain control, or recording volume. This control sets up the machine to cope with a range of amplitudes, so it is important to set up the reference point (0 dB) at the highest amplitude of the subject's range. This should be done manually, *not* via any automatic gain control that the recorder may have. Tatham (1984) suggests that the subject might produce a 'test word', such as *cart*, which contains the /ɑ/ vowel, generally considered to have one of the highest intrinsic amplitudes. The gain control can then be set so that the meter needle touches 0 dB on that test word, and this should then suffice for this subject. Naturally, this control must then remain unaltered for that recording session.

Conclusion

In this chapter we have attempted to explain how a tape recorder captures a speech signal and how to maximize the accuracy of this process. With clinical data even more so than with normal speech, it is essential we get as good a recording as possible whether for transcription or acoustic analysis, as we cannot prejudge which phonetic features are important for any eventual description and which are simply incidental, particularly in the speech clinic.

Further reading

There has not been a great deal written in the phonetics literature about recording speech, despite the fundamental importance of this procedure for many kinds of speech analysis. The one important contribution to this area has been referred to during the chapter: Tatham (1984).

CHAPTER 17

Acoustic Analysis: The Spectrograph

The recorded speech signal needs to be analyzed if we wish to find out information as to its acoustic make-up. Since the late 1940s in acoustic phonetics the instrument that has mainly been used in this task is the sound spectrograph; indeed Fry (1979, p.76) describes this as an 'indispensable item of equipment in the phonetics laboratory'. The first sound spectrograph is described in a paper by Koenig, Dunn and Lacy (1946), and although many changes and developments have taken place to the apparatus described there, the basic functions of the machine are the same. In recent years computerization has lead to an increase in the efficiency and applicability of the spectrograph, and these developments will be outlined briefly later in the chapter. However, this chapter does not attempt to be a manual in the use of the spectrograph, but rather to explain what it does and how it does it.

Analyzing frequency

The spectrograph is able to produce in diagrammatic form the spectra of speech sounds, which were described in Chapter 15. In order to do this, and to produce so-called three-dimensional spectrograms (see below) it must be able to analyze the speech signal into its component frequencies for subsequent display. It achieves this through the use of filters.

We saw in Chapter 15 that filters are a 'by-product' of resonance: if a resonator amplifies certain frequencies, it also 'filters out' the other frequencies of a complex wave. We can therefore construct electronic filters (resonance circuits) that pass frequencies within a certain band of frequencies, but greatly reduce the energy of frequencies outside this band. These 'band-pass' filters can be set to different frequencies, and have differing 'band widths' (i.e. the size of the band of frequencies that they pass).

In one mode, the spectrograph has a bandwidth of 45 Hz. To visualize how this would work in the frequency analysis of a speech signal, we can envisage a bank of filters tuned to different 45 Hz bandwidths right across the spectrum. The funda-

Figure 17.1 Spectrogram of /ɑ/ and /i/ with narrowband power spectrum on upper left taken at the cursor. Frequency divisions, 500 Hz

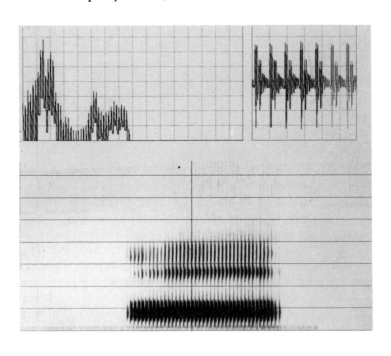

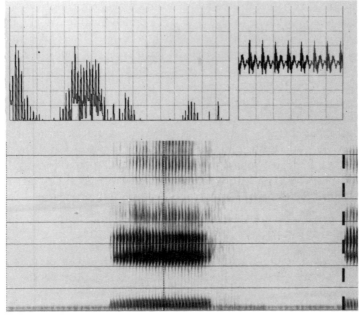

mental frequency of the sound will be registered by one of the filters, and its amplitude measured. Similarly, the harmonics will be 'passed' by the relevant filters. All other filters will register no energy, and so measure no amplitude. In this way the spectra of the sound will be measured. In fact the spectrograph does not use a bank of filters, but a single filter that is continually retuned to look at the bands of frequency selected.

Spectra displays such as those in Figure 17.1 show frequency on the horizontal axis against intensity in dB on the vertical. These spectra are selected from a single moment in time during a speech sound, and are given the name 'section'. They clearly show the first three formants of the sounds (where the intensity is greatest, see Chapter 15), but they tell us nothing about what is happening during the speech event; in other words the dimension of time is excluded.

The spectrograph, however, can be put into a mode whereby time is included in the analysis: this produces the so-called 'three-dimensional' spectrogram. The picture produced in this mode has time along the horizontal axis (with most instruments a maximum of 2.4 sec can be recorded at any one time, though this can be doubled by the use of a larger recording drum), and frequency along the vertical axis (in the usual setting the range of frequencies displayed is 0–8000 Hz, though other ranges can be selected). Intensity is shown by the darkness of the trace on the resultant spectrogram (see Figure 17.2). The darker the trace, the greater the intensity. Naturally, this only gives a qualitative impression, not a measurable one.

We have already noted that in one mode the spectrograph employs a band width of 45 Hz, and this band width is well adapted to produce sections of the type illustrated in Figure 17.1. This is because a narrow band width filter system is sharply tuned (see Chapter 15) and gives maximum frequency information. It is not so efficient when time is included, as in three-dimensional spectrography. This is because the sharply tuned system is only lightly damped, so it takes time before new information can be dealt with; at 45 Hz band width this time gap is 20 msec, so speech events following within this gap (and important features, such as voicing, are shorter than this) are lost.

To overcome this the analysis can be done with a wider band width. The one commonly used for speech analysis is 300 Hz. Although this does not provide such accurate information on frequencies, it gives better time resolution at about 3 msec.

In most work in acoustic phonetics we are more interested in changes in time than in precise frequency information, so 'broad-band' (or 'wide-band') spectrograms are those most commonly encountered. Figure 17.2 shows the difference between 'broad-' and 'narrow-band' spectrograms for the same sound. While the narrow-band example clearly shows individual harmonics (the horizontal markings), the broad-band one shows the individual pulses of vocal-fold vibration (voicing: the vertical striations). Admittedly, the frequency information is less clear in the broad-band example, but the formant structure is easy to ascertain, and this is what the acoustic phonetician is most interested in (see Chapters 18–22 below).

Figure 17.2 (a) Narrow and (b) broad band spectrograms of the word 'car'. Frequency divisions, 1000 Hz

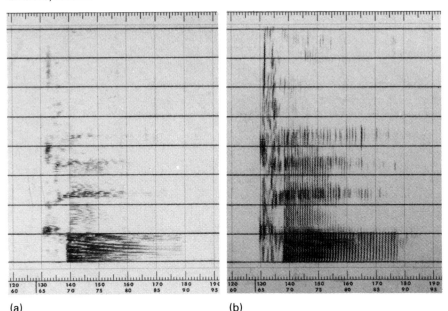

(a)   (b)

Analyzing intensity

We have seen above that intensity can be analyzed in dB in the 'section' mode of speech spectrography, or in a qualitative manner in three-dimensional spectrograms. A combination of a dB measurement and the time dimension is also available via the 'amplitude display'.

The amplitude display is usually added to a normal three-dimensional spectrogram, replacing the top or bottom part of the analysis. It shows a continuous trace of the intensity of the components of the utterance, whose frequency analysis is shown in the other part. Such a display is given below in Figure 17.3.

Analyzing noise

We noted in Chapter 13 that sound waves could be periodic or aperiodic. So far in this chapter we have only considered periodic speech sounds, whose noise source is the vocal-fold vibrations from the larynx. On the other hand, some speech sounds may consist partly or wholly of aperiodic 'noise' (such as fricatives, voiceless sounds, whispered speech).

Figure 17.3 Amplitude and waveform display of 'Shakespeare'. Frequency divisions, 1000 Hz

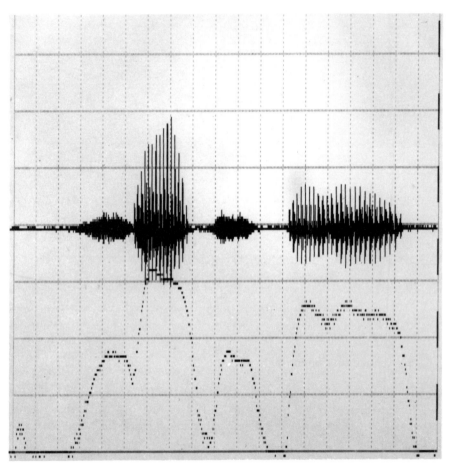

Acoustically, noise is 'a continual switching from one frequency to another over a wide range of frequencies throughout the duration of the noise' (Fry, 1979, p.103). This is shown on the spectrogram by a wide and relatively undifferentiated distribution of markings over a range of frequencies. However, even aperiodic speech sounds do concentrate their acoustic energy within certain limits, so, for example, [s] has little or no energy below about 4000 Hz, while [ʃ] has energy down to about 2000 Hz. It is these distinctions that allow us to distinguish the aperiodic sounds of speech, and we return to this aspect of analysis in Chapter 18.

The spectrograph and disordered speech

The spectrograph has been used to study almost every speech disorder found in the clinic. A full description of this range of studies (and, indeed, the therapeutic uses of the instrument) is available in Farmer (1984). She includes in her account studies of stuttering and cluttering, the dysarthrias, aphasia and apraxia of speech, hearing impairment, voice disorders, and even language disorders. In the following chapters we will be describing some of the findings of spectrography with disordered speech with reference to different aspects of the speech signal.

Conclusion

The spectrograph has proved to be one of the most useful instruments invented for the acoustic phonetician; the literature on its use in speech analysis is vast. However, we must exercise care in the treatment of spectrograms, in that complete accuracy is never possible. In the first place the various mechanical restraints of recording and playback naturally affect the signal, and the measurements we can take from the resultant spectrograms also have constraints of accuracy whether we consider time or frequency. Fry (1979, pp. 108–10) discusses some of these in some detail.

Figure 17.4 A modern real-time spectrograph: The Kay DSP Sonagraph 5500

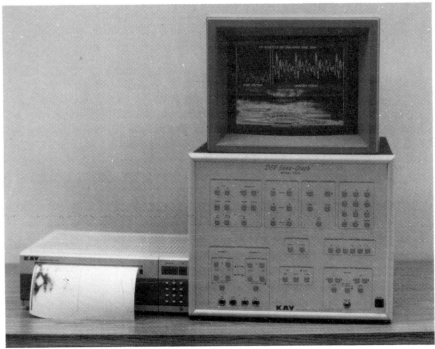

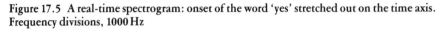

Figure 17.5 A real-time spectrogram: onset of the word 'yes' stretched out on the time axis. Frequency divisions, 1000 Hz

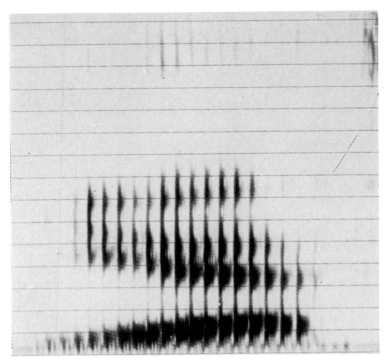

Recently, there have been major developments in sound spectrography. This has led to the introduction of computerized real-time analysis. Figure 17.4 pictures one of these types of spectrograph, while Figure 17.5 is one of the spectrograms obtained from such an instrument.

In the following chapters in this Part we will be looking at the acoustic characteristics of normal and disordered speech, concentrating on the evidence available from spectrographic studies.

Further reading

The history of the development of spectrography can be traced through papers in Lehiste (1967), in particular Koenig, Dunn and Lacy. Texts such as Fry (1979) devote a considerable time to describing spectrography and results obtained from the technique; in particular chapter 9 of this book is worth consulting. As noted above, Farmer (1984) is the best overview of spectrography in disordered speech research.

CHAPTER 18

Acoustic Characteristics of Vowels and Diphthongs

Vowels

As with all speech sounds, the precise acoustic characteristics of vowels differ from speaker to speaker, and with one speaker from moment to moment. However, despite these differences, the overall acoustic envelope (see Chapter 15) of the different vowel phonemes of a language will remain constant across utterances. For this reason we can present mean values of, for example, vowel formants derived from the analysis of numerous speakers.

The first acoustic characteristic that is common to vowels in almost all languages in non-disordered speech is that they are voiced (the voiceless vowels of, for example, French are linguistically marginal). This means that, as with other voiced sounds, there are clear bands of high energy visible on the spectrographic record: the *formants*. Indeed these formants generally are used by acoustic phoneticians to classify vowels rather than frequency–intensity spectra of the sort shown in Figure 17.1, though these latter are of course also helpful when we wish to examine relative intensities more thoroughly.

Most vowel articulations have three clear formants, though it is arguable that the first two of these (working upwards in frequency) are the clearer indicators of vowel quality, as the third remains relatively constant. In acoustic descriptions of speech sounds these formants are generally abbreviated as F1, F2, and F3, and should we need to refer to the fundamental frequency this is usually shown as F0.

We noted in Chapter 17 that wide-band spectrograms are most suitable for speech work. On such wide-band spectrograms the vowel formants appear as broad, dark bars running the width of the vowel sound. Such bars are clearly seen on the spectrograms of a selection of English vowels reproduced in Figure 18.1. The figure also shows that as we move from high-front to low-front vowels F1 rises in frequency and F2 lowers. With the back vowels, as we move from low to high we find that F1 and F2 maintain a mostly similar distance, but both move back down the frequency range. Figure 18.2 shows this change in diagrammatic form. Central vowels have F1 and F2 quite high in frequency, thereby (as expected) being between the acoustic characteristics of the front and back vowels.

Figure 18.1 Wideband spectrograms of the English vowels / ɑ, i, u, e, ɪ, æ /. Frequency divisions, 1000 Hz

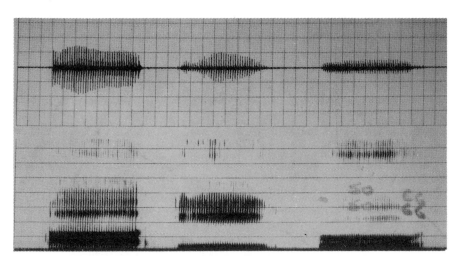

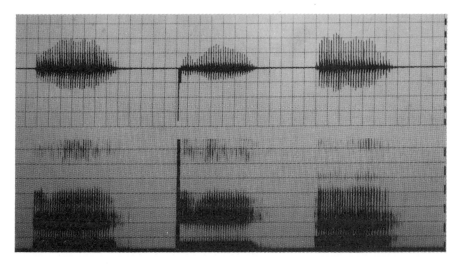

Peterson and Barney (1952) undertook a major study of vowel acoustics, and in Table 18.1 are reproduced the results of their investigation of seventy-six speakers: men, women and children. The vowels investigated are of the General American accent, and relative intensities as well as formant and fundamental frequencies are shown.

Figure 18.2 Formant values for vowels. Frequency divisions, 1000 Hz

Table 18.1 Average of fundamental and formant frequencies and formant amplitudes of vowels by seventy-six speakers. (Source: Peterson and Barney, 1952)

		i	ɪ	ɛ	æ	ɑ	ɔ	ʊ	u	ʌ	ɚ
Fundamental frequencies (Hz)	M	136	135	130	127	124	129	137	141	130	133
	W	235	232	223	210	212	216	232	231	221	218
	Ch	272	269	260	251	256	263	276	274	261	261
formant frequencies (Hz)											
F_1	M	270	390	530	660	730	570	440	300	640	490
	W	310	430	610	860	850	590	470	370	760	500
	Ch	370	530	690	1010	1030	680	560	430	850	560
F_2	M	2290	1990	1840	1720	1090	840	1020	870	1190	1350
	W	2790	2480	2330	2050	1220	920	1160	950	1400	1640
	Ch	3200	2730	2610	2320	1370	1060	1410	1170	1590	1820
F_3	M	3010	2550	2480	2410	2440	2410	2240	2240	2390	1690
	W	3310	3070	2990	2850	2810	2710	2680	2670	2780	1960
	Ch	3730	3600	3570	3320	3170	3180	3310	3260	3360	2160
formant amplitudes (dB)	L_1	−4	−3	−2	−1	−1	0	−1	−3	−1	−5
	L_2	−24	−23	−17	−12	−5	−7	−12	−19	−10	−15
	L_3	−28	−27	−24	−22	−28	−34	−34	−43	−27	−20

M: men, W: women, Ch: children

Vowels of course differ in length as well as in terms of formant frequencies. As noted in the previous chapter, it is possible to measure the length of segments from a spectrogram, but some caution is needed. Firstly we must remember that for both mechanical reasons and the difficulty of accurate measuring, precise amounts of time cannot be calculated. Also we must bear in mind that the segmentation of speech into discrete sounds is only a convenient fiction as the various aspects of speech production do not have co-occuring 'boundaries'. It may therefore be difficult to fix initial and final points between which to measure the length of a vowel. Finally, length of a vowel (or any segment) will also depend on phonetic environment, and the speech rate of the speaker.

Nevertheless, by examining a large number of speakers and taking mean values, it becomes clear that some English vowels are longer than others. For example, [i], [ɑ], [ɔ] and [u] are longer than [ɪ] [æ], [ɒ] and [ʊ]. Table 18.2 demonstrates this (adapted from Peterson and Lehiste, 1960).

Table 18.2 Durations of vowels in American English

Vowel	Average for five speakers (msec)
i	240
ɪ	180
eɪ	270
ɛ	200
æ	330
ə	230
ɑ	260
ɔ	310
oʊ	220
ʊ	200
u	260
aʊ	300
ɑɪ	350
ɔɪ	370

It can also be seen that all vowels in English have different lengths dependent on the following consonant. Lenis (or voiced) consonants generally have longer preceding vowels than do fortis (or voiceless) ones. This feature is returned to in Chapter 22.

This section has concentrated on the acoustic characteristics of English vowels. Formant values for other vowels have been investigated and, for example, those of the primary and secondary cardinal vowels are given in Delattre, Liberman, Cooper and Gerstman (1976, p.225).

Diphthongs

As discussed in Chapter 9, diphthongs are vowel sounds which involve a movement of the articulators during the production of the sound. Acoustically this is manifested as a change in the formant structure during the diphthong.

Figure 18.3 shows spectrograms of some of the common diphthongs of English, and it can be seen that the formant structures at the beginning and at the end of these diphthongs are similar to those of the respective 'pure' vowels (monophthongs). By investigating the time dimension, it will be seen that the English diphthongs are similar to long vowels in this respect.

An acoustic analysis of diphthongs can sometimes help the phonetician to decide the most appropriate form of transcription. If, for example, the final part of a closing diphthong resembled the formant structure of [ɪ] rather than [i], then a transcription of (say) [aɪ] might be better motivated than one of [ai].

Figure 18.3 Wideband spectrograms of English diphthongs: 'bay', 'buy', 'bough'. Frequency divisions, 1000 Hz

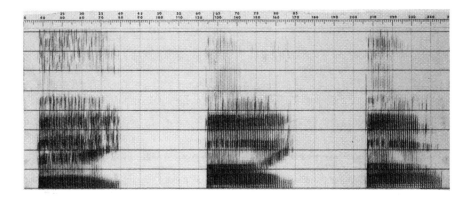

Disordered speech

As noted in Chapter 9, disordered speech cannot produce vowel sounds outside the 'vowel area', but nevertheless vowels (or diphthongs) outside the range expected in the language concerned may well occur. In such cases impressionistic transcription often proves difficult, even for those trained in the Cardinal Vowel System (see Ladefoged, 1967). Acoustic analysis of such vowels via the spectrograph may well help the clinician to decide more clearly what kind of vowel articulations are being produced by the patient.

In patients suffering from velopharyngeal insufficiency (see also Chapter 7), vowel articulations will demonstrate hypernasality. Spectrographically this appears as a characteristic 'nasal formant'. This is discussed in more detail in the next chapter, but examples of nasalized vowels are given in Figure 18.4 below.

Figure 18.4 Oral and nasalized vowels: [ɑ,ɑ̃] – [ɔ,ɔ̃]. Frequency divisions, 1000 Hz

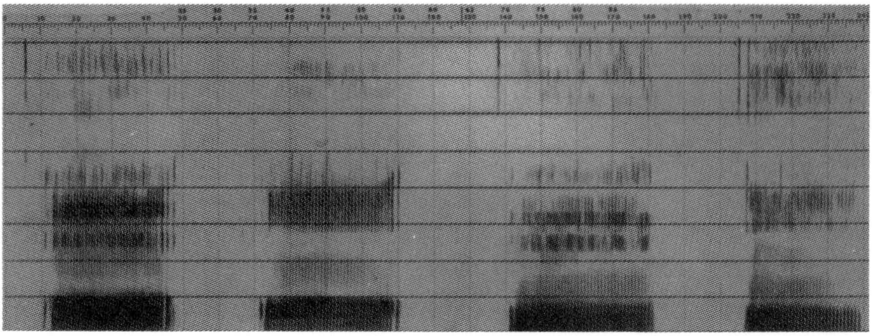

Spectrography can also be used as a way of measuring intensity and length in the vowel sounds of disordered speech. Code and Ball (1982) used the fact that vowel lengths differ before fortis and lenis consonants (see above) to investigate a patient with apraxia of speech. This speaker appeared to lack the voicing contrast in intervocalic fricatives, but spectrography showed (among other features) that the vowel length differences were mostly being maintained despite the lack of vocal fold vibrations. The problem appeared, then, not to be a phonological one of the loss of one class of consonants, but a phonetic planning one of coordinating this contrast.

Further reading

The references contained in this chapter are sufficient for readers who wish to follow up specific topics to do with vowels and diphthongs. Fry (1979) chapter 10 contains details on these sounds as part of an introductory account of speech acoustics, whereas Lehiste (1967) and Fry (1976) contain contributions exploring this area in more detail. Fry (1976) also contains an interesting contribution (by Paget) on a prespectrographic attempt to investigate the acoustics of vowels.

CHAPTER 19

Acoustic Characteristics of Sonorants

We saw in Part I of this book that consonants can be classified according to manners of articulation such as stop, fricative and approximant. Another classification exists, strongly influenced by work in acoustic phonetics: sonorant versus obstruent. Sonorants are in many respects vowel-like acoustically, and so it is logical to consider them next. In traditional terms they consist of approximants (median and lateral), e.g. semi-vowels (or 'glides') and liquids, and nasals. Sounds like trills and taps are of a somewhat controversial status in this regard, most authorities (e.g. Lass, 1984) treat them as sonorants, but they clearly share many acoustic characteristics of obstruents (= non-sonorants).

Glides

As their alternative name — semi-vowels — suggests, glides are acoustically very similar to vowels. As described in Chapter 5, these sounds are momentary in that the articulators move away immediately to take up the position required for the following sound. This is also visible on the spectrographic record (see Figure 19.1), where we can see that the formants for the semi-vowel show an immediate transition towards those of the following vowel. The acoustic characteristics of the initial, glide-part of these utterances show that [j] and [w] are very similar to [i] and [u] respectively, and indeed some authorities (e.g. Fry, 1979, p.114) suggest that acoustically glides followed by a vowel are very much like the reverse of diphthongs (see Chapter 18).

The amount of time the glide transition takes depends of course on many factors such as overall speaker tempo and so on. However, it is generally longer than the formant transitions between a nasal consonant and a vowel (perhaps four times as long). This is necessary from a perceptual viewpoint: for the listener to be able to identify this transition as a 'segment' of the language.

Figure 19.1 Wideband spectrograms of glides: 'win, yes'. Frequency divisions, 1000 Hz

Liquids

Liquid is a cover term for lateral approximants and median ones of the typical English 'r' variety [ɹ]. Other sounds such as lenis non-fricative continuants of the [ʋ] and [ð̞] type, and trills and taps may also be found under this heading, but we will be concentrating here on the sounds [l] and [ɹ] as used in English. These two sounds are similar in some ways to the glides that have just been described, however the patterns of formant transitions for these sounds show that they take place somewhat more rapidly than do those for the glides.

Figure 19.2 shows spectrograms of [ɹ] and [l] in prevocalic position. They are seen to be vowel-like acoustically in that they both demonstrate formant structure, but they are comparatively shorter than the surrounding vowels. [ɹ] in most English accents has some degree of retroflexion, and this can clearly be seen in the formant transitions where there is a move towards and then away from a retroflex-vowel formant pattern. This is most noticeable in the behaviour of F3, which lowers and then rises again during the articulation of this sound. [l] does not demonstrate this change in F3, but we do see changes in F1 and F2 where there are quite abrupt transitions. The precise nature of the formant transitions with [l] (and indeed with [ɹ]) depend to some extent on the preceding and following sounds, but the behaviour of F3 is constant here: it changes for [ɹ] but not for [l].

Another feature about [l] that is important is the difference between clear- and dark-l. Many English accents have a clear-l allophone ([l]) before vowels, and a dark-l allophone ([ɫ]: velarized) after vowels or before consonants. Inappropriate

Figure 19.2 Wideband spectrograms of liquids: 'late, rob'. Frequency divisions, 1000 Hz

usage of such allophones may feature in clinical experience, and acoustic evidence may be helpful to see more clearly what differentiation if any is being used. The difference between the two l-qualities reflects closely the difference between front and back vowel qualities.

Acoustic descriptions of trills and taps are not included here, but may be found, for example, in Jassem (1962).

Nasal consonants

As we saw in Chapter 7, nasal consonants involve the blocking off of the oral cavity, with the sound being emitted solely through the nasal cavity. The result of this is a lowering of intensity in nasal sounds, as can be seen in the spectrograms of nasals in Figure 19.3, where the traces for the nasal segments are quite faint. In 'reading' spectrograms of these consonants it is often more useful to examine what happens

Figure 19.3 Wideband spectrograms of nasal consonants: 'Mom and Nancy are running'. Frequency divisions, 1000 Hz

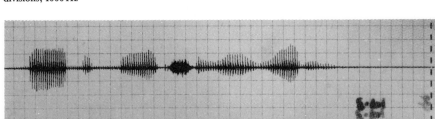

to the surrounding vowels than to attempt the analysis of the nasal consonant segment itself.

The acoustic characteristics of nasals result from the change to the vocal tract noted above. As noted in Fry (1979, p.118), the main effect is the introduction of an antiresonance (or filter) in the frequency range of 800–2000 Hz. If we compare the nasal segment to a neighbouring vowel we find that this antiresonance results in the F1 of the consonant being quite a bit lower than in the vowel (it is also less dark on the spectrogram, but this is because nasals have a lower intensity as already noted), and that the F2 band for the vowel is virtually or completely missing for the nasal consonant. These two features are shown in Figure 19.3. The lowered first formant is often termed the 'nasal formant', and the band of antiresonance has been termed the 'antiformant'.

Examining the nasal consonants themselves on broad-band spectrograms gives little information as to how they differ (though see Jassem, 1962, and Delattre, Liberman, Cooper and Gerstman, 1976, for more details here). However, an examination of the transitions between the nasals and surrounding vowels helps here, in particular the behaviour of the vowel's F2. For the alveolar nasal F2 involves relatively little transition, whereas for bilabial nasals we see a transition to a lower frequency if before a nasal, and from a lower frequency if after a nasal. The velar nasal involves F2 transition to or from a higher frequency. Other nasal consonants are described acoustically in Jassem (1962). In Chapter 18 we included a spectrogram (Figure 18.4) of nasalized vowels. It will now be seen that these nasalized vowels have the characteristic antiresonance noted above.

We can conclude this section with Fujimura's (1962, p.1874) remarks on nasal consonants:

The perceptual impression of nasal sounds is somehow substantially different from that of other speech sounds. It is reasonable, therefore, to assume that there are some gross acoustic features that characterize the nasals as a class. In view of our data concerning the structure of the spectral envelope, it may be said that the following three features characterize the spectra of nasal murmurs [i.e. sounds] in general: (1) the existence of a very low first formant that is located at about 300 cps [= 300 Hz] and is well separated from the upper formant structure; (2) relatively high damping factors of the formants; and (3) high density of the formants in the frequency domain (and the existence of the antiformant).

Disordered speech

Naturally, as we saw in Part I, there are numerous ways in which sonorant consonants may be affected in disordered speech, and we will be able to concentrate on only one in this chapter. One common substitution feature (or phonological process, see Grunwell, 1987) involving approximants is often termed 'liquid gliding', that is the substitution of a glide for a liquid. The most common of these in English involves the replacement of target /r/ (i.e. phonetically [ɹ]) by some kind of labial approximant. Often this is the glide [w], but also common is the lenis continuant [ʋ]. [w] and [ʋ] are impressionistically very close, and although visual cues can help us distinguish the bilabial from the labiodental articulation, acoustic information can be an important additional aid in deciding what a patient is using. The spectrograms in Figure 19.4 show the three sounds [ɹ], [w] and [ʋ], demonstrating a visual method of attempting to distinguish these approximants.

Figure 19.4 Wideband spectrograms of [ɹɑ], [wɑ] and [ʋɑ]. Frequency divisions, 1000 Hz

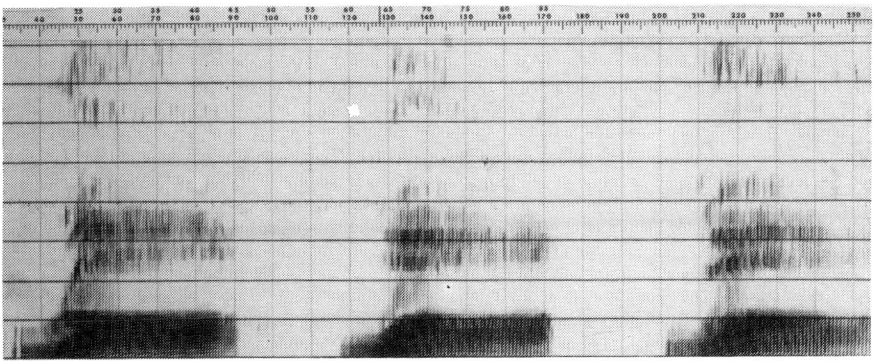

Further reading

The important references on the spectrography of sonorants are mostly included in this chapter, and many of them are contained in the collections edited by Lehiste (1967) and Fry (1976). As noted previously, Fry (1979) provides a good introductory account to the spectrography of speech, even though it concentrates on English.

CHAPTER 20

Acoustic Characteristics of Obstruents

The term obstruent includes what we termed in Chapter 5 plosives (oral stops), affricates and fricatives. From an articulatory viewpoint these all involve an obstruction (complete or nearly so) to the airflow somewhere in the oral cavity. From an acoustic viewpoint it can be seen that they differ from vowels and sonorants in that they lack a clearly defined formant structure and/or are accompanied by aperiodic wave forms ('noise'). In this way, spectrograms of obstruents are clearly different from the preceding speech sounds.

Plosives

As described in Chapter 8, plosives are marked by having a complete closure in the oral tract, with the result that the acoustic record will display a measurable period of silence corresponding to this closure. On a spectrogram, silence is shown by the absence of any marking throughout the frequency range, therefore all plosives will be accompanied by such a blank section on a spectrogram. Care must be taken here, however, as a blank section on a spectrogram will not always mean a plosive is being marked, as affricates (see below) also have this feature, and of course it may well correspond to simple pauses in the utterance in question.

Another feature that will help us identify plosives is the plosive burst (though this will be absent in unreleased, laterally released and nasal released stops: see Chapter 8). This burst of noise is relatively short for unaspirated plosives, but longer for aspirated ones, and on spectrograms often commences with a thin vertical marking running up through the frequency range. For the rest of the burst the noise is distributed through different frequency ranges dependent upon the place of articulation, Figure 20.1 shows these differences. For bilabial plosives the noise is generally distributed through frequencies around 600–800 Hz, for velars around 1800–2000 Hz, and for alveolars around 4000 Hz.

Figure 20.1 Wideband spectrograms of plosives: 'paul, tall, call, beer, deer, gear'. Frequency divisions, 1000 Hz

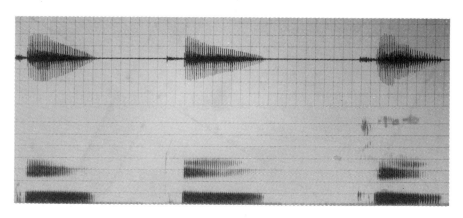

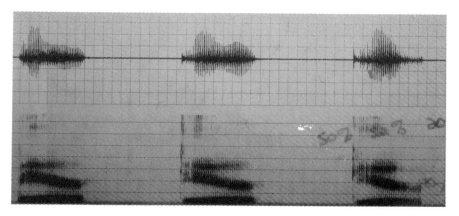

Other acoustic aspects we should examine are intensity and time. As with all other consonants, the lenis (or voiced) plosives have less intensity than do the fortis ones. On wide-band spectrograms as in Figure 20.1 this is seen in the paler markings, though of course section analysis or an amplitude display (see Chapter 17) would show this more exactly.

In terms of time, the lenis plosives are generally shorter than the fortis in both the silent component and the noise burst. The silent part of the plosive can last between about 70 msec and 140 msec, with the lenes being at the shorter end of this range and the fortes at the longer. The noise burst is quite short in the lenis stops, perhaps around 10 to 15 msec, while with aspirated stops it can reach 50 msec though the precise length here is related to place of articulation. Amount of aspiration is language-, and to some extent speaker-specific, and sometimes considerable amount of aspiration (even preaspiration, commencing before the plosive burst) may occur.

Even with the information already noted, it is not always easy to determine place of articulation from the spectrographic record. Formant transitions between the plosives and neighbouring sounds in connected speech can be a help here, and will be returned to in Chapter 22. Details of non-English plosives are not included here, but may be found for example in Jassem (1962).

Fricatives

Whereas the noise component of a plosive is a relatively short one, and only part of the acoustic make-up of the sound, that of a fricative lasts throughout the sound and is the main information we have as to the identity of that sound. We saw in Chapter 17 that noise is distributed across the frequency range, but depending upon the shape of the vocal tract, this distribution will be restricted to certain ranges of frequency. Figure 20.2 shows some of the fricatives found in English, and it will be seen that the noise component of these appears as markings at different levels on the spectrograms.

Figure 20.2 Wideband spectrograms of fricatives: 'foot, thought, sail, shoe, vase, there, zoo, beige'. Frequency divisions, 1000 Hz

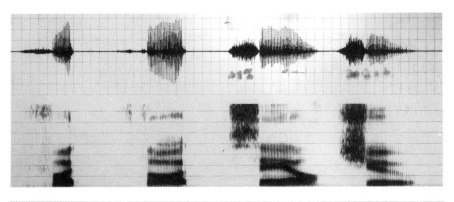

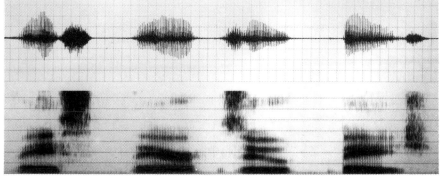

On average, [ʃ] has noise between 1900 Hz and 6000 Hz; [s] between 4000 Hz and 8000 Hz; [f] and [θ] between 6000 Hz and 8000 Hz. These last two, then, are not readily distinguishable acoustically in terms of their noise components alone, but as we will see in Chapter 22, the formant transitions between neighbouring sounds and these fricatives can help in this respect. [h], although acoustically similar to fricatives in that it contains a noise component, can be thought of as a voiceless onset to a following vowel. This is born out in the acoustic record, as spectrographic analysis usually shows that [h] segments contain a formant structure close to or identical with that of the voiced vowel sound which it precedes.

Spectrographic analysis can also demonstrate differences between fortis and lenis fricatives. Generally, lenis fricatives are shorter than their fortis counterparts and their intensity is less. This latter point is important as often this lack of intensity means that the noise component is only faintly represented, or totally absent from the spectrogram. This is particularly true of speakers who use very weak, almost approximant, articulations of lenis fricatives.

Details of non-English fricatives are not included here, but may be found, for example, in Jassem (1962), Strevens (1960) and Hughes and Halle (1956).

Affricates

In articulatory terms affricates are a combination of a stop closure and a fricative release. In acoustic terms too, these sounds share features of both plosives and fricatives. Spectrographically, then, the record shows a period of silence, very much of the same length as with the plosives, followed by a noise component longer than that of aspirated plosives, though shorter than that of a simple fricative.

The friction components of affricates are similar acoustically to the comparable fricative; that of [tʃ], therefore, has a noise component in the range 1900 Hz upwards, while that of [tɻ], ([ɻ] is a retroflex fricative similar to the continuant [ɹ]

Figure 20.3 Wideband spectrograms of affricates: 'chase, jaw, true, drape'. Frequency divisions, 1000 Hz

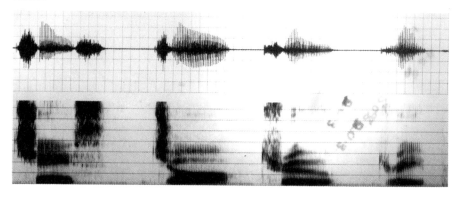

described in Chapter 19) has a retroflex quality, in the range of 1200 Hz upwards. These two affricate types are shown in Figure 20.3.

Differences between fortis and lenis affricates are of the same type as described for the previous two sound classes: a lower intensity and shorter duration for the lenis sounds as compared to the fortis.

Disordered speech

As described in Part I, sounds of the obstruent type are subject to numerous varieties of disorder involving place and manner of articulation, voicing, length, repetition, etc. The information in previous chapters may help sort some of these out from the acoustic viewpoint.

Figure 20.4 Wideband spectrograms of disfluency: 'his name is Pete', with disfluency at the onset of 'Pete'. Frequency divisions, 1000 Hz

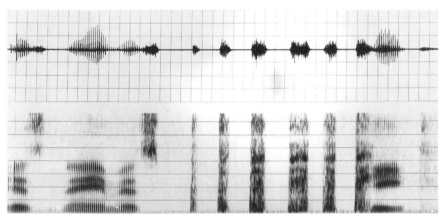

Figure 20.5 Wideband spectrograms of ejectives: [p'a], [tʃ'a], [s'a]. Frequency divisions, 1000 Hz

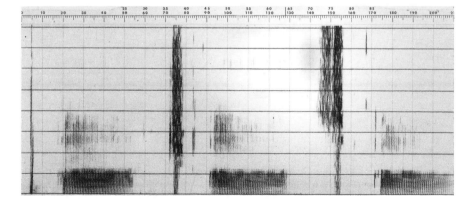

However, we will examine spectrograms of two types of disordered speech in this overall category of obstruent: disfluency and ejective stops/fricatives (these latter are not disordered in some languages). These are illustrated in Figures 20.4 and 20.5, from which we can see the characteristic aspects of the acoustic signals of these two different speech types.

Further reading

Again, any important further reading is referenced during the chapter. Farmer (1984) discusses the application of spectrography to the analysis of disfluent speech.

CHAPTER 21

Acoustic Characteristics of Suprasegmentals

As we noted in Chapter 11, suprasegmental aspects of speech are generally considered to include length, stress and pitch (or intonation). In the previous chapters of this Part, we have addressed the topic of length while examining the acoustic characteristics of 'segmental' speech. The length of individual speech sounds (insofar as we can identify them), or of longer stretches of speech can be measured quite easily and fairly accurately from the spectrographic record.

Stress is generally considered to be an amalgam of various phonetic features, mainly length, intensity and pitch movement. Length, as just mentioned, can be calculated relatively easily, and intensity can of course be measured spectrographically in a number of ways: qualitatively via three-dimensional spectrograms, or via a section or an amplitude display. The third aspect, pitch, can also be investigated spectrographically, though other instrumental techniques have also been developed in this area which can produce clearer results. Pitch in terms of intonation studies will be investigated in some detail in the next section, but we can note here that acoustic studies of stress are reported in, amongst others, Fry (1976), and Lehiste (1970).

Intonation

What we perceive as intonation are the pitch changes caused by alterations in the rate of vocal-fold vibration. In acoustic terms these changes manifest themselves as alterations to the fundamental frequency (F0) of the speech signal.

It is possible, though not completely straightforward, to measure F0 from spectrograms, and various studies (for example Lehiste and Peterson, 1961) have done this. As we saw in Chapter 17, narrow-band spectrograms give the clearest readings when we are concentrating on frequency rather than time, and clearly show the harmonics of a sound. While the fundamental frequency is often not very clear on a spectrogram, from the harmonics it is quite an easy matter to calculate the

F0. Lehiste and Peterson (1961) employed this method, and comment (p.379, note 3):

> The fundamental frequency was derived by measuring the center frequency of higher harmonics on a 4 in. narrow-band spectrogram; the measured frequency was divided by the order number of the respective harmonic to obtain the fundamental frequency. Usually, both the 10th and the 20th harmonics were measured. On these spectrograms 0.1 in. represents about 88 Hz, and the individual harmonics are considerably narrower. Calibration tones and repeated measurements show the accuracy to be within ± 20 Hz, and in the region of the 20th harmonic this represents an accuracy of ± 1 Hz.

This kind of study has provided us with some important information regarding the behaviour of F0 in speech. For example the Lehiste and Peterson study just mentioned concluded that intonation levels perceived as the same will in fact be marked by different F0 levels acoustically. It appeared that factors which controlled the choice of 'allotones' (i.e. the precise acoustic quality of the particular intonation 'toneme') included the quality of the syllabic sound (that is the sound on which the intonation level is operating) and the quality of the consonant preceding this syllabic sound. Differences due to stress were also observed, as were inter- and intra-speaker variations.

However, spectrographic studies of intonation suffer from the fact that, apart from being somewhat difficult to read, they are limited in terms of time. The use of narrow-band analysis, as noted in Chapter 17, does compromise temporal accuracy, but more importantly traditional spectrography is limited to the analysis of speech samples of 2.4 sec (or 4.8 sec with a larger recording drum). Through the use of short utterances we may well be able to examine individual intonation 'tunes' within this time limit, but to get a picture of how it operates over longer stretches of discourse we need to turn our attention elsewhere.

Pitch instrumentation

Currently spectrography is probably no longer the most popular way to examine the acoustic characteristics of intonation. Whereas it needs extremely complicated instrumentation to examine the entire acoustic spectrum of speech, to extract solely the fundamental frequency is not such a difficult operation. Therefore, we have seen an expansion in the number of instruments designed just for this function, and many of these are not available 'off-the-peg', in that they have been designed on a 'one-off' basis by a particular phonetics laboratory for a particular piece of analysis or experimentation.

This development can be seen, for example, in a collection of recent studies on intonation by Johns-Lewis (1986). In several of the papers the authors describe their own instrumentation constructed or adapted for the specific investigation. So Jassem and Demenko note (p.9):

The instrumentation which we are using is a hybrid system. It includes a Tonometer; a pitch extractor (or 'detector') . . . ; an extremely simple mini-computer . . . ; an interface designed in our laboratory; and an ordinary TV receiver. The special interface (called Memoskop) is able to produce on the screen of a commercially available TV receiver, a graphic representation of digital information stored internally or externally. An F0 trace is also obtained in the form of a printout together with the measurement of instantaneous pitch (in Hz) at time intervals that can be set to a variety of values . . . or in the form of a graph on the TV screen, with variable time and frequency scales.

An alternative bank of instruments was used in Johns-Lewis' contribution: 'The speech signal was fed through a 12 bit analogue to digital converter to a mini-computer installation' (p.210), and Graddol also notes the use of a 'micro-computer based installation which was designed and built for the purpose' (p.223).

However, many clinical phoneticians and speech pathologists will not have access to this kind of equipment, and in recent years we have seen the development of commercially available instruments that can be used in investigating intonation. One such is the electrolaryngograph which displays pitch changes as well as rate of vocal fold vibrations. The laryngograph was described in Chapter 12, as we included it under the heading of articulatory instrumentation. Of course, although it does measure the articulatory activity of the vocal folds, it can also display the acoustic information of pitch changes. However, another recent development that is specifically designed to show pitch, and indeed to have clinical applications, is the Visi-Pitch™, and we will examine this device in the next section.

Visi-Pitch™

The Visi-Pitch™ instrumentation is produced by Kay Elemetrics, the main manufacturer of spectrographs (under the trade name of Sonagraph™). This piece of equipment is designed to provide instantaneous feedback (a 'real-time' display) about pitch, voice quality and amplitude/intensity. The more recent versions have added functions, allowing, for example, the use with the Visi-Pitch™ of the laryngograph discussed in Chapter 12. The machine has been mainly aimed at the speech pathologist, though it has applications in several other areas as well, and one feature of particular use to clinicians is the 'split-screen' facility, which enables one display (for example the speech pathologist's) to be retained to be compared with a second (the patient's).

A wide-range of speech disorders have been investigated by the Visi-Pitch™, including intensity-related voice disorders, voice-quality disorders (such as vocal fry), glottal attack (or inappropriate voice onset), and motor speech disorders. These last can be the result, for example, of dysarthia or apraxia of speech, and as prosodic features are often crucial in distinguishing these two factors, the equipment can be particularly useful in making a diagnosis.

Other features that can be distinguished via this instrumentation include oesophageal speech (see Chapter 2). The Visi-Pitch™ can be used as a monitoring device in this case to determine how well the patient is progressing with learning the technique of the oesophageal air-stream mechanism.

A whole range of suprasegmental errors and problems are often present in deaf speech. Because of the visual feedback the instrument provides, this is a particularly useful approach not only to diagnosis but also to therapeutic intervention with deaf speakers. Aspects such as pitch levels, intensity, voice quality, pausing and prolongation, and stress can all be tackled this way.

Recent versions of the Visi-Pitch™ have been designed to interface with microcomputers, some of which can do statistical analyses of the results obtained in experimental work. The machine can also be linked to printers to provide hard copy of the traces displayed on the screen. Figures 21.1 and 21.2 show examples of such printouts: Figure 21.1 is of a normal speaker whereas Figure 21.2 shows the use of the instrument in the clinic, with a patient attempting to copy a preset pitch pattern.

Figure 21.1 Visipitch traces: intensity curve (upper trace), pitch curve (lower trace)

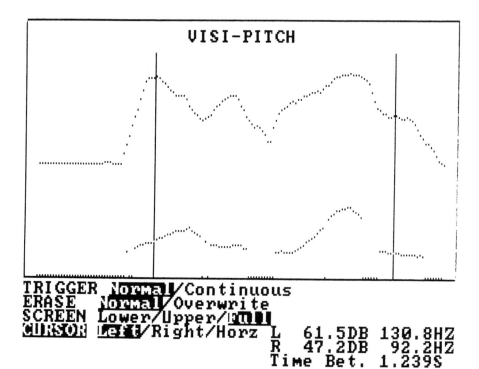

Figure 21.2 Visipitch traces: split screen display showing a model pitch curve (upper trace) and the patient's attempt to copy it (lower trace)

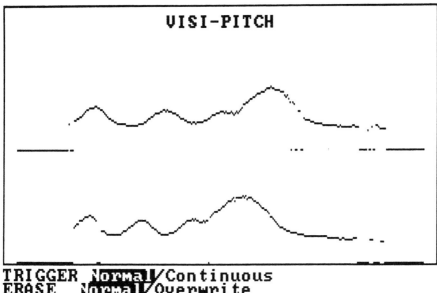

Further reading

The most important survey of suprasegmentals is Lehiste (1970); however, this is not really an introductory text. The other works referenced during this chapter can also be consulted of course, but there is a lack of an introductory account of suprasegmentals and acoustic analysis.

CHAPTER 22

Acoustic Characteristics of Connected Speech

In Chapters 18–20 we looked at the acoustic characteristics of vowels and consonants as displayed through spectrography, but in most cases in a static manner, that is to say as if the segments were discrete units. But we have stressed in several places that the speech signal does not in fact operate like this, and in Chapter 11 we looked at some of the assimilations (or 'coarticulations') that occur in connected speech. In this chapter we will look at the acoustic correlates of some of these, and see that in many respects it is these features that help us identify the different parts of the speech signal, both in terms of the spectrographic record and, indeed, in terms of speech perception (though this latter point will not be considered in detail until Chapter 28 in Part III). While looking at the acoustic correlates of coarticulations we should bear in mind that disruptions to these patterns can severely affect intelligibility, as much as do changes to the individual 'segment' features.

Coarticulation

Coarticulation is a term employed by acoustic phoneticians to describe the modifications that occur to speech sounds due to influences from neighbouring acoustic events (and is therefore similar to the articulatory phonetician's term 'assimilation'). Fant (1973) notes in this respect: 'A common observation when spectrograms of ordinary connected speech are studied is that modifications and omissions of speech sounds are frequent. Carefully pronounced single testwords and phrases may differ considerably from ordinary speech' (p.19).

Fant illustrates this by examining the spectrogram of the phrase 'Santa Claus' as pronounced by an American subject (though most of the comments would hold true for other accents of English). The impressionistic transcription of this is given as [sǽntə klɔːz], and this is compared to the spectrographic record. Among other things this showed anticipatory nasalization of the [æ] vowel which is evident right through the formant structure of the vowel, being shown by the characteristic 'split' first formant. The [t] segment appears to virtually disappear, though as Fant points out: 'alternatively, it might be argued that there is no separate [n] segment, the intended /n/ being signified by the nazalisation of the [æ] and of the following voiced nasalized dental stop [d̃] (p.21).

Fant goes on to discuss alternative views as to the nature of continuous speech. He outlines four differnt approaches: firstly, that speech is a sequence of ideal non-overlapping phonemes; secondly, that it is a sequence of minimal sound segments with boundaries defined by relatively distinct changes in the sound wave structure; thirdly, that one or more sound features characterizing a sound segment may extend over several segments; and finally that speech contains a continuously varying important function for each phoneme describing the extent of its dependency on particular events within the speech wave, lacking sharp boundaries (Fant, 1973, p.21). These differing approaches are illustrated in Figure 22.1.

Figure 22.1 Sequential elements of speech

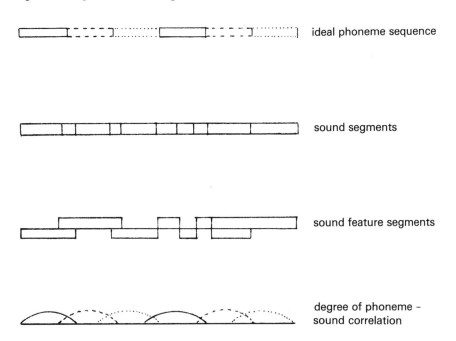

ideal phoneme sequence

sound segments

sound feature segments

degree of phoneme –
sound correlation

These four approaches are not, however, mutually exclusive and all have a part to play in any attempt to analyse speech. The first, discrete phoneme, approach is that adopted by the phonologist (or, indeed, graphologist) and accounts for the way in which speech is organized mentally as the message level of representation. The second and third views relate directly to what we know about the acoustics of the speech signal: some acoustic features (such as the change from voice to noise) have sharply defined boundaries, while others (such as formant transitions) do not.

The final approach perhaps goes some way to account for the way in which speech sounds are perceived (though perception of speech is dealt with in detail in Part III).

Coarticulation, then, can be seen to exist within the framework of a set of otherwise discrete sound segments, though these sound segments may not have a one-to-one correspondence with what we think of as phoneme segments. To some extent, coarticulations are speaker/speech event specific; for example, the amount of vowel nasalization in the context of nasal consonants, or word-final devoicing etc., is variable. However, some researchers have argued (see for example Öhman, 1966, 1967) that there is a basic tendency towards some amount of coarticulation for all speakers. Öhman gave evidence that in articulations the precise physical gesture of the tongue is always affected to some extent by preceding and/or following sounds. In the acoustic signal these effects are seen as formant transitions.

Formant transitions

Much work within acoustic phonetics has been aimed at discovering which aspects of the speech signal are important in speech perception. Some of these perception experiments are described in Chapter 28, but as part of the background to these studies, investigators concentrated on examining those aspects of connected speech where the acoustic signal behaved differently from sounds when they were considered in isolation. As we have already noted, the area of formant transitions soon came to the fore.

One of the early investigations into this aspect was conducted by Delattre, Liberman, Cooper and Gerstman (1976, though published initially in 1954). They describe it as 'the transition between consonant and vowel, seen . . . as a curvature of the formants during the vowel onset' (p.315). The authors feel that such shifts in the formants are a reflection of the movements of the articulators as they go from one position to another, and therefore that it would be expected 'to find these shifts in the region where two phones join' (p.316).

This and other studies found that formant transitions, particularly of F2, could in general be associated with place of articulation (and thereby form an important acoustic cue for the perception of place differences by listeners). Delattre *et al* summarize the findings on F2 transitions in CV (consonant–vowel combinations) as follows (Delattre *et al.*, 1976, p.316):

> The movement of the second formant is typically upward when the vowel follows /p/ or /b/; after /t/ or /d/ the second formant of the vowel starts at a position 'near the middle of the pattern', with the result that this formant will then rise or fall depending on whether its normal, steady-state position in the vowel is higher or lower than the /t-d/ starting point; after /k/ or /g/ the second formant starts at a position slightly above its steady-state position in the vowel, wherever that may be, and the transition is always, therefore, a relatively small shift downwards.

As noted in Chapter 19, such transitions also occur with nasal stops, and of course similar changes occur with all consonants. The role of formant transitions in speech perception is considered in Part III (see Chapter 28).

Clinically, we find in some cases that normal coarticulatory effects are missing or reduced. This is particularly so with speakers who use a markedly reduced speech tempo, or who pause excessively between parts of an utterance. Various pathologies may give rise to this (e.g. apraxia of speech, aphasia, disfluency), but the results can, of course, be examined acoustically via spectrography, and modifications to formant transitions and so on can be seen.

Voice quality

A different aspect of connected speech (arguably under the heading of suprasegmentals, though the previous chapter was restricted to intonation) is voice quality. We outlined in Chapter 3 the various phonation types found in normal and pathological speech, and we can now briefly discuss the acoustic correlates of some of these.

Two such phonation types that can be found used normally and as part of disordered speech when used inappropriately are creak (and creaky voice) and whisper. Fry (1979) describes creaky voice (also known as 'vocal fry') as showing in acoustic terms a very low fundamental frequency, and being characterized 'by the interspersion of larynx cycles of abnormally long duration' (p.68). These cycles may also be found alternating with cycles of shorter period 'so that there is a short cycle followed by a long cycle, followed by a short cycle and so on' (p.68). Creaky voice is likely to be found with a fundamental frequency of between 20 and 60 Hz.

Although fundamental frequency may not be straightforwardly observed spectrographically (see the previous chapter), a broad-band spectrogram will show in the spacing of the vertical striations the slower rate of vocal-fold vibrations. Figure 22.2 shows the phrase 'how are you?' pronounced with creaky voice.

Whisper in acoustic terms involves the replacement of the periodic sound source of voiced phonation with an aperiodic noise source at the same location. However, as long as there is enough energy, this noise source is as capable as the periodic voice source of producing the resonances in the vocal tract needed for intelligible speech. This means that vowels still display their characteristic formant patterns (see Figure 22.2), but accompanied by less intense energy across a wide range of frequencies.

Studies of pathological voice have looked at a wide range of voice-related disorders. Some of these have a clear physiological cause in that the vocal folds may be damaged in some way, though with others the exact cause may be difficult to assess or may be linked to psychological factors. Whatever the causes, a range of voice qualities from hoarseness to breathy have been described. Acoustically these all have typical patterns, but it is beyond the scope of this chapter to examine these in detail. Readers are recommended to consult Laver (1980) and Moore (1971).

Figure 22.2　Wideband spectrogram of creaky voice: 'how are you'. Frequency divisions, 1000 Hz

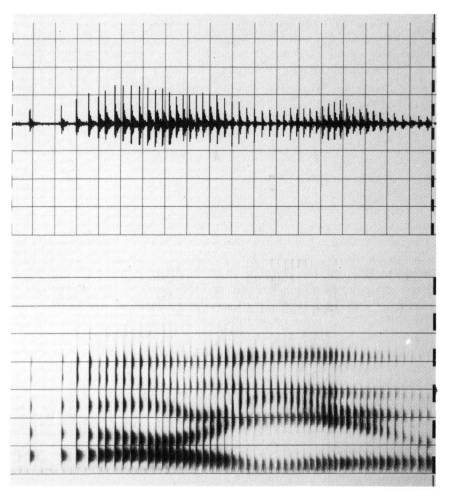

Finally in this chapter we will look at a feature of voice quality sometimes encountered clinically that is more to do with initiation than with phonation. Most normal speech is uttered on a pulmonic egressive air stream but, as noted in Chapter 2, other air streams can also be used. Most of these can only be used to produced very short stretches of speech (usually a single segment), but a pulmonic ingressive air stream can be used for relatively long utterances. As stated in Chapter 2, this air stream is not used in normal speech apart from a few exceptional instances, but it can be found in disordered speech. An example of pulmonic ingressive speech is given in Figure 22.3, which can be compared with pulmonic egressive speech in previous figures.

Figure 22.3 Wideband spectogram of pulmonic ingressive speech: 'one, two, three'. Frequency divisions, 1000 Hz

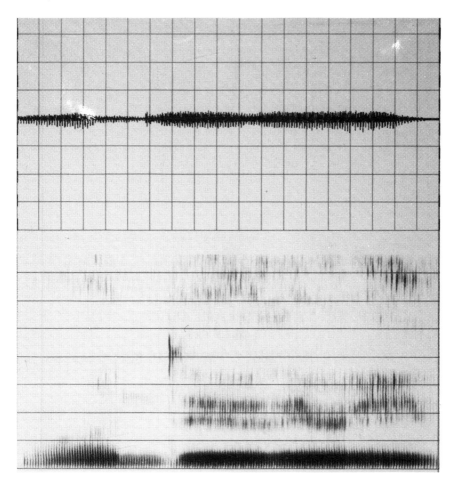

Further reading

The most important reference for the first part of this chapter is Fant (1973), though it should be noted that this is not an introductory text, and may be felt to be 'heavy reading'. Likewise, Laver (1980) is the recognized text on voice quality, and again requires a good deal of phonetic knowledge to gain the best from it. Fry (1979) does provide a fairly straightforward description of formant transitions in his chapter 11.

PART III
Auditory Phonetics

CHAPTER 23

Hearing: The Ear

Just as in Part I when considering articulatory phonetics we had to look at the vocal organs which produce speech, so in this part when considering auditory phonetics we have to look at the parts of the body that receive sound: the ear and the auditory system. However, auditory phonetics is not simply the study of the 'mechanics' of the ear. Coupled to this aspect of hearing is perception: the neural activity in the brain that transforms the hearing activity in the ear into something which we can (or sometimes cannot) understand. In this and following chapters we will look at these three stages of hearing: the ear, perception and comprehension (i.e. the linguistic aspects of auditory phonetics).

The auditory system is often divided into two parts: the *peripheral auditory system* (the various parts of the ear), and the *internal auditory system* (the neural and brain activity). The first of these systems is described in this chapter, the second in Chapter 24.

The outer ear

Despite what we might expect from the name 'outer' (or 'external') ear, the term is not restricted to the visible part of the ear, but includes the ear canal and the ear drum as well (see Figure 23.1). The convoluted folds of skin on either side of the head ('the ear' in common parlance) is known as the *pinna*. This structure is relatively immobile in humans, though of course in many animals it can be moved to aid in locating sound sources and/or maximizing the concentration of sound waves into the ear canal.

The ear canal, or *external auditory meatus*, is a hollow cylindrical tube about 2.5 cm long, and is air-filled. This canal of course acts as a resonator (see Chapter 15), and has a natural frequency between 3000–4000 Hz (depending upon the individual), and therefore amplifies those sound waves near its resonant frequency. The result of this is that the ear appears very sensitive to sounds at this frequency.

Figure 23.1 Overall view of the ear

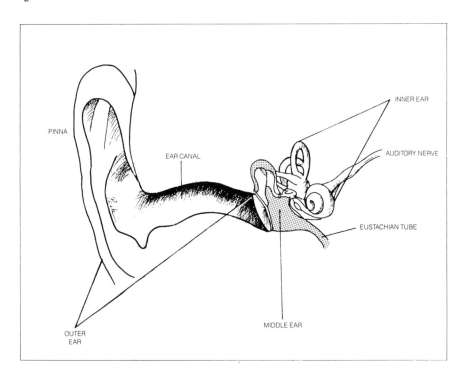

The ear canal is terminated at its inner end by the ear-drum, or *tympanum*. This is a somewhat conical membrane, having an area of about $0.75 \, cm^2$, and is about $0.01 \, cm$ thick. Sound waves falling on the pinna are funnelled down the canal, and set the ear drum into vibration. It is extremely sensitive to air-pressure variations, and if the frequency of this variation is near the resonant frequency, it will detect a variation of one ten-thousand-millionth of the atmospheric pressure. The location of the tympanum clearly serves two purposes: firstly as a protection against physical damage that it might suffer if located externally, and secondly to enable the resonator effect of the meatus to boost sound waves that would not have otherwise been perceptible.

The middle ear

The middle ear (see Figure 23.2) is also filled with air, being about $2 \, cm^3$ in volume. Contained within this cavity, and attached to its walls by ligaments, are three auditory ossicles: the *malleus*, the *incus* and the *stapes* (also known as the 'hammer, anvil and stirrup'). The handle of the malleus is attached to the inner surface of the tympanum, and covers over half of the area of the ear-drum. As the three ossicles

Figure 23.2 The middle ear

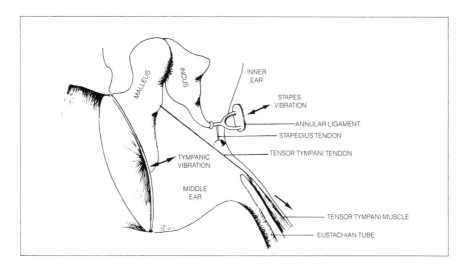

are all connected and articulate with each other, movements from the tympanum are transmitted through the malleus, the incus and the stapes. The 'footplate' of the stapes covers the *oval window* (the entrance to the inner ear), so in this way vibrations of the ear-drum can be passed through the middle ear to the inner ear.

We noted earlier that the middle ear is an air-filled chamber, but that it is sealed from the outer ear by the tympanum. To avoid pressure differences between the outer and middle ear becoming so great as to cause distortion to the ear-drum there needs to be an opening from the middle ear to the outside air to aid the equalization of pressure. This outlet is the *eustachian tube* which connects the middle ear to the oral cavity (effectively the outside air). Many of us will have experienced the discomfort of pressure differences between the middle and outer ear, as when taking off or landing in a plane. If we swallow, this allows the eustachian tube, which is normally closed, to open briefly and equalize the pressure. Large differences in pressure can cause great pain, and even damage to the ear-drum.

The purpose of the middle ear is two-fold: the increase of the acoustic energy to be sent to the inner ear, and the protection of the inner ear from loud sounds. The amplification activity of the middle ear is undertaken in two ways. The lever mechanism of the ossicles produces a greater force at the oval window than was applied at the ear drum: an increase of about a factor of 1.5. Secondly, the more important way concerns the fact that the force applied by the stapes is applied to a much smaller area (the oval window, or *fenestra*) than the origin of the force: the ear-drum. The ear-drum is about twenty-five times greater in area than the oval window. If we combine these two factors, we can work out that the pressure at the oval window is about thirty-five times greater than would be the case if the tympanum led immediately into the inner ear.

The protective function of the middle ear involves various actions to reduce the amount of pressure transmitted to the oval window in the case of very loud sounds. One way involves the pulling in of the tympanum, and the disconnection of the stapes from the oval window by muscular activity, while another involves a change in the mode of vibration by the ossicles above certain frequencies of excitation — again, decreasing the pressure variations transmitted to the inner ear. While quite efficient, these methods are not instantaneous, so sudden loud noises can cause damage to the inner ear.

The inner ear

The most important part of the inner ear is the *cochlea* (see Figure 23.3), as it is here that the transformation takes place from physical movement to neural impulses in hearing. The cochlea looks somewhat like a coiled snail's shell, and is divided internally into two main parts along most of its length by the cochlear partition: a membraneous structure whose interior forms a third region (see Figure 23.4).

Figure 23.3 The cochlear portion of inner ear

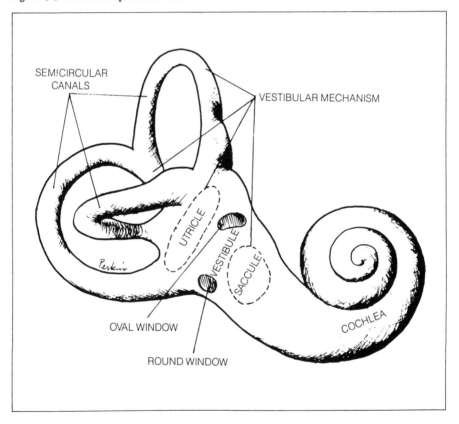

Figure 23.4 A longitudinal section of the unrolled cochlea

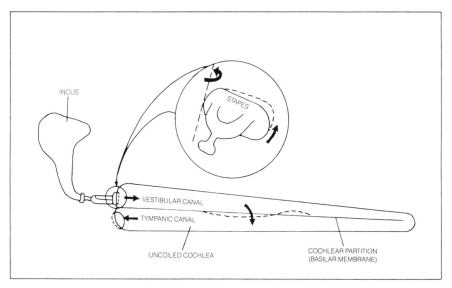

One of the two main partitions ends (at the basal end) at the oval window; this region is called the *scala vestibuli*, the other being the *scala tympani*. They are connected at the apical end by the *helicotrema*, and this allows *perilymph*, a viscous fluid with which both regions are filled, to flow between the two. The scala tympani ends (at the basal end) at the round window (see Figure 23.2), and is also connected with the perilymph-filled vestibular canals, but these have no function in hearing.

Pressure variations from the middle ear arriving at the oval window cause movements in the perilymph which pass through the scala vestibuli, the helicotrema, and back through the scala tympani, and eventually cause movement at the round window. This activity, however, is too slow to deal with sound vibrations; for these we must look at the actions of the partition between the two scala.

This partition has a hollow centre (see Figure 23.5), the *cochlear duct*, which is filled with an even more viscous fluid: *endolymph*. The boundary between the duct and the scala vestibuli is formed by *Reissner's membrane*, while the *basilar membrane* separates it from the scala tympani.

Also improtant is the bony shelf shown in Figure 23.5. At the cochlea's basal end, the basilar membrane is narrow, and the bony shelf extends practically right across. Near the apical end the shelf is practically non-existent, and the membrane covers most of the space between the cochlear walls. There is, then, a gradual change in the width of the basilar membrane from 0.04 to 0.5 mm. This difference has an important role to play in the hearing process. When sound waves are received at the oval window, and cause changes in the perilymph, they also cause movement to the entire cochlear partition. However, because of the differences

Figure 23.5 Cochlear canals

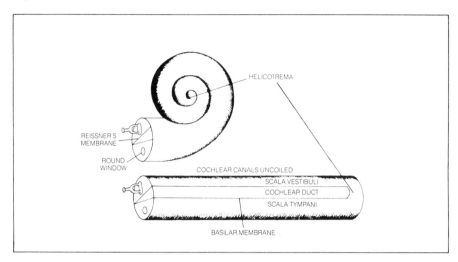

noted above, the amplitude of vibration at different points along the partition depends on the applied frequency. For example, high frequencies cause greater partition vibration near the oval window, low frequencies nearer the helicotrema.

The final conversion of this activity into neural impulses takes place in the *organ of corti* (see Figure 24.1). Within this organ are hair cells, resting on the basilar membrane. Fine hairs link these cells to the *tectorial membrane*. Vibratory changes in the basilar (and so also the tectorial) membrane are transmitted to these hair cells. In turn, nerve fibres from the auditory nerve (which are located near to the hair cells) take these movements as eletrochemical pulses to the auditory centre of the brain. This process is described in more detail in Chapter 24.

Further reading

There are, of course, many books on aspects of hearing, but in this section I will concentrate on those that are within the phonetic tradition. Many phonetic texts do not cover auditory aspects of speech, but a good exception to this is Brosnahan and Malmberg (1970), chapter 9, and O'Connor (1973), chapter 4. Perhaps one of the best accounts is to be found in Denes and Pinson (1973) chapters 5 and 6. The anatomy and physiology of hearing is covered well in Perkins and Kent (1986), chapters 9, 10 and to a lesser extent 11, and this publication contains its own lists of further readings in the area.

CHAPTER 24

Hearing: Perception

In the previous chapter we examined the working of the peripheral auditory system, and we will follow this by looking at the internal auditory system. In doing this we will not only account for how sound is perceived, but we will look also at what aspects of sound humans can perceive and how we measure these aspects.

The internal auditory system

The internal auditory system consists basically of the auditory nerve and its connections, and the relevant part of the brain: the auditory projection area on the temporal lobe of the cerebral cortex. It is still not quite clear precisely how the physical movements in the cochlea are converted into neural (i.e. electrochemical) impulses along the auditory nerve, though we do have a general notion of how this works. The receiving parts of the nerve are called 'receptor neurons', and there are about 28,000 in each ear. These are located in the *spiral ganglion* parallel to the organ of Corti (see Figure 24.1).

From the spiral ganglion, dendritic extensions run into the organ of Corti, and their endings form a synaptic connection with the hair cells. It is assumed that the movement of different hair cells on the basilar membrane results in differential stimulation of these extensions of the receptor neurons, which in some way causes the neurons to 'fire'. As with other neural pathways, the auditory nerve does not lead directly from the inner ear to the brain: it contains connection points (or 'synapses') along the route where the bundles of fibres meet other such bundles.

We need not describe here in detail the path taken by the auditory nerve (see for example Denes and Pinson, 1973, pp. 139–40), though we can note that the main synaptic connections occur at the *cochlear nucleus*, the *super olivary complex*, and the *medial geniculate body*. At these points it is probable that some kind of information processing takes place, particularly as the number of incoming fibres does not always match the number of outgoing ones.

Figure 24.1 The organ of corti and a sectional view of the cochlea

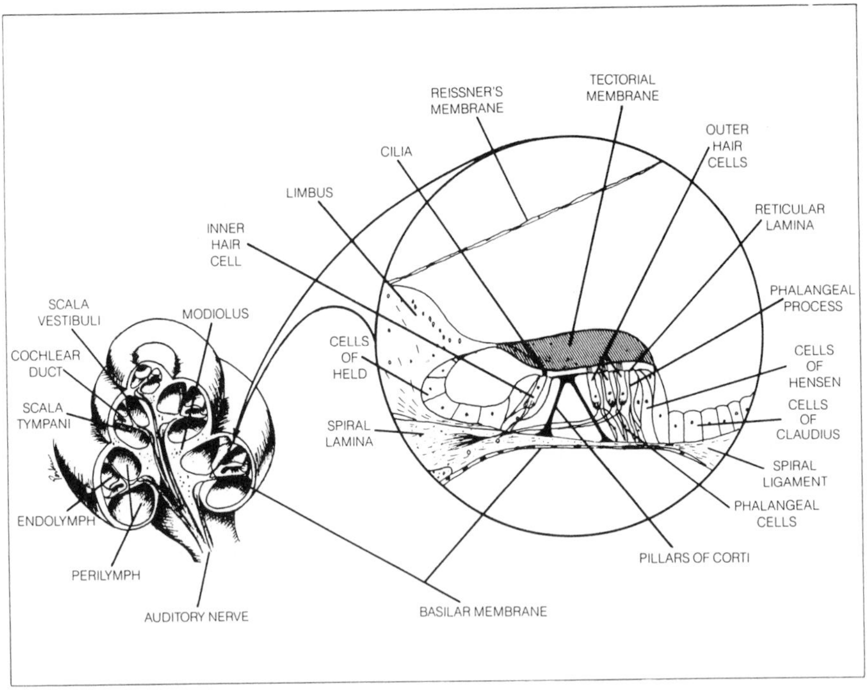

Finally, we need to note that reverse pathways exist from the brain to the ear as part of the elaborate feedback system, described more fully in Chapter 29.

Another area of uncertainty in auditory phonetics concerns how hearing operates in the brain. Various theories of hearing have been proposed (see Denes and Pinson, 1973, pp. 141f), but current thinking is that, while there is still a lot to be understood, we can work with a topographical model (see Brosnahan and Malmberg, 1970, p. 166). This approach states that sound waves of differing frequencies will disturb different hair cells in the basilar membrane. In turn, different fibres in the auditory nerve will be stimulated along all its stages, resulting in projection to different parts of the auditory area in the cortex. This approach claims, therefore, that we perceive different sound frequencies topographically: because they are projected to different parts of the hearing section of the brain.

If the perception of pitch is related to which fibres carry pulses to the brain, it is thought that the perception of loudness is related to the total number of pulses reaching the auditory area per second; as the more intense the sound the larger the number of pulses that are transmitted.

The inner auditory system, however, cannot be solely analyzed topographically. There is evidence to suggest that the brain can calculate fundamental frequencies even when they are physically not present (e.g. in certain complex waves). Also, some researchers feel that the cochlea is incapable of the fine degree of frequency analysis to account for what we know is possible in the auditory system. Clearly, there is still plenty to investigate in the area of auditory perception.

Aspects of perception

Apart from studying how sounds are perceived, the auditory phonetician is particularly interested in examining what sort of sounds can be perceived by humans. This is a finite area: humans cannot perceive the whole range of possible sound waves. To demonstrate this we need only think of the specialist dog whistles that emit a very high pitched note, too high for us to hear but not for the dog; or of the 'radar-like' high pitched cries of bats, most of which we cannot perceive. Much of this work centres on levels of hearing acuity (i.e. loudness) and on the perception of pitch. We must bear in mind, however, that experimental work in this area (sometimes called 'psychoacoustics', see Chapter 28) is of necessity less objective than that in articulatory or acoustic phonetics, as we are asking subjects to report on their own internal sensations.

One area where we do have good data is the investigation of the limits of hearing: that is to say the sounds which are within the range of frequency and intensity perceptible to normal hearing. We measure this by utilizing sounds of different frequencies, discovering the intensity (in dB) at which they can just be heard, and using this as a lower limit. We can then establish an upper limit at the threshold of feeling: that is to say a dB level that begins to cause the subject pain or discomfort.

Using this framework we find an average perceivable frequency range in young people of 20–20,000 Hz, though this falls to 20–12,000 Hz in the over-sixties. The maximum sensitivity for perceiving sound is 3000 Hz.

The range of intensities the human ear can cope with comfortably differs according to the frequency concerned, and this is best displayed in diagrammatic

Figure 24.2 The limits of hearing

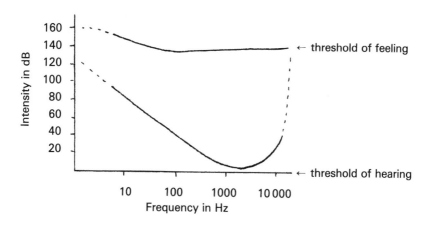

form, as in Figure 24.2. Not all these frequencies can be used for speech, however. Rarely will any speaker use frequencies less than 125 Hz or more than 8000 Hz, though speech will still sound normal if filtered to a range of 200–4000 Hz. Telephone systems generally compress this further still (say 400–2400 Hz) which is why certain sounds are notoriously confusable on the phone (e.g. /f/ – /s/) as they possess important distinguishing characteristics in the upper frequencies.

The measurements we have looked at so far are physical ones, but in psychoacoustic work various subjective scales have been devised (see Chapter 13 for initial discussion of the Mel scale). These scales are used to try to demonstrate what the listener actually perceives.

In loudness studies use is sometimes made of the *phon* scale. This scale is used to show the perceived loudness level of a sound independent of its physical intensity. That is to say that sounds of different frequencies but the same intensities may not sound identically loud, or conversely, sounds of different frequencies and different intensities may sound equally loud. Figure 24.3 shows how these factors relate to one another in the phon scale.

Figure 24.3 The Phon Scale: the curves are labelled with loudness levels in phons

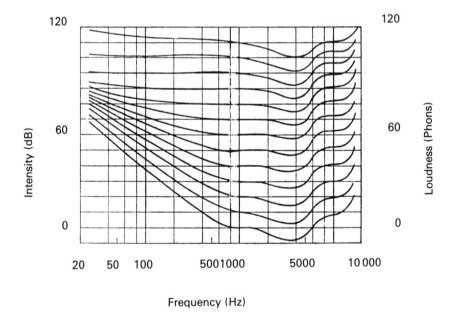

Frequency (Hz)

Figure 24.4, on the other hand, shows a numerical scale for loudness (the *sone* scale) in relation to the phon scale. This numerical scale (as opposed to the intensive scale of the phon system) works in the following way: a listener judges a sound of two sones to be twice as loud as a sound of one sone, and so on.

Figure 24.4 The Sone Scale: perceived loudness in sones depends upon the loudness level of the stimulus in phons

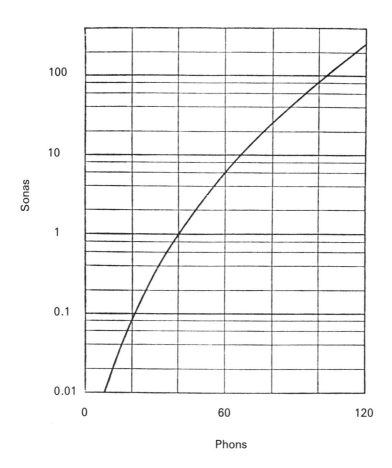

Phons

A similar numerical scale exists for pitch: that is the perception of frequency differences. This is the Mel scale, with which listeners judge whether a sound is twice / half the pitch of another sound, and so on. A graph showing the relationship between frequency in Hz, and perceived pitch in Mels is given in Figure 24.5.

The final perceptual area we will examine is concerned with thresholds of hearing. Not the absolute thresholds of hearing, which were discussed earlier, but the relative thresholds of distinguishing one sound from another. This is termed the *difference limen* or *just noticeable difference*, and can be examined in terms of frequency or intensity.

We have not got the space here to go into this in great detail, as difference limens are not constant and vary according to the intensity / frequency in question.

Figure 24.5 The Mel Scale: subjective pitch in mels is related to frequency in Hz

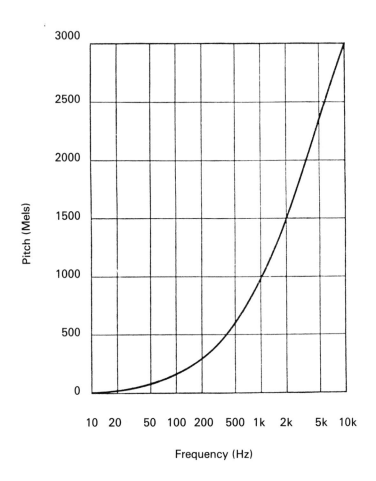

We can, however, give some examples. A tone of 1000 Hz at 5 dB must be doubled in intensity (to 10 dB) before a difference is noticed; however an identical tone at 100 dB needs only a 6% per cent increase for this to be noticed.

Measurements have also been made on the minimum necessary frequency changes to be noticeable. It appears that for moderate intensities, a frequency change of 2 to 3 Hz is necessary in frequencies below 1000 Hz.

In this section we have been able to look at some of the features of sound perception. In Chapter 28 we will look again at psychoacoustic experimentation in perception and how this has given us a better idea of the important aspects of the acoustic speech signal.

Further reading

The references given at the end of the previous chapters will also have information relevant to the study of perception; again, Denes and Pinson (1973) is particularly useful.

CHAPTER 25

Hearing: Comprehension

In this chapter we intend to look at the final link in the hearing chain: comprehension. That this is different from perception is easy to demonstrate. Many of us will have had the experience of tuning in to a foreign radio station (perhaps by accident) broadcasting in a language with which we are unfamiliar. We can hear the language used (that is to say, we perceive the sounds), and may even be able to recognize some or all of the sounds used, but we do not understand the message: we cannot comprehend the signal we receive. In the following sections we will examine, then, how listeners comprehend what they hear.

Modelling comprehension

The modelling of how the brain comprehends, or understands, a spoken (and by analogy, a written) message is necessarily a speculative, and controversial, field of study. We can, however, be fairly certain of the outline of the process of comprehension, even if we cannot be sure of the detail.

In outline, then, we can envisage a system whereby the phonetic input that is perceived via the peripheral and internal auditory systems is matched to a set of 'phonetic templates' stored in the brain on a quasi-permanent basis. If a match is found, then the word or phrase (or whatever combination of morphemes or words the utterance might be stored under) is understood. If no match is found, then the word or phrase is rejected by the listener and comprehension breaks down. Now, although we have stated that this is a grossly oversimplified model, there are some points that we can profitably raise. For example, how close a match need there be between input and template for the input to be accepted? Also, how much detail of the phonetic make-up of potential inputs is held in the template? Let us now examine these two related points.

Even the most basic knowledge of how speech works is enough to tell us that there must be an amount of leeway or flexibility between the input and the template. Unlike a voice triggered electronic lock that can be 'trained' to respond

150

to only one speaker, humans must be able to understand a wide range of speakers, and single speakers under a range of physical or emotional states or background noises. A single vowel or consonant is probably pronounced very slightly differently each time it is used (even in the same word when repeated) by a single speaker, and in everyday communication we often encounter many speakers, more so since the advent of mass electronic communication.

Apart from individual differences, most of us are also able to understand speakers of different dialects than our own. Therefore the template must not be too rigid (or perhaps separate templates are set up, marked as a particular dialect) or we would, for example, accept [bʌs] and reject [bʊs] for 'bus' (or vice versa). The fact that usually we do not accept one and reject the other demonstrates the ability of the brain to cope with varieties of speech. Of course, we realize that these forms do come from separate accents, and we often assign 'social' meanings to these differences.

However, there are limits. Many of us will be familiar with instances when a very marked (often called 'broad') local accent has caused confusion, or even communicative breakdown. A good example is quoted in Trudgill (1986, p. 23), showing confusion between American accents (waiter), and British (Trudgill):

> Waiter: Would you care for another bottle of wine?
>
> Author: A half bottle, please.
>
> Waiter: Coffee?

The problem was of course that the /a ː/ in *half* sounded to the waiter more like his own vowel in *coffee* than the expected /æ/ vowel of *half*.

From this it can be seen that if the input is too far removed from the guidelines provided in the template, a match may not be made or, as in this instance, an incorrect match may be constructed.

We noted earlier that we cannot state for certain whether these 'templates' are in the form of syllables, words or phrases. Evidence from slips of the tongue would suggest that in articulatory planning the syllable is an important unit, but also groups of words. This is because often the slips take place between adjacent words, but involve the same place in syllable structure. An example might be: 'I hought I theard John' /aɪ hɔt aɪ θɜd dʒɒn/. There would be a good chance that someone hearing this utterance would correctly identify it as: 'I thought I heard John' /aɪ θɔt aɪ hɜd dʒɒn/, though they would most probably (though not necessarily) realize that a mistake had been made. Nevertheless, this is evidence that in comprehension, as in production, the brain is able to work with units of various sizes, and to make connections between them.

On a smaller scale, too, we can see the brain's abilities to cope with incorrect inputs. Presented with an input such as: /kɑz wə pɑkt ɔl əlɒŋ ðə stvit/ (British RP pronunciation) in the majority of cases listeners will claim to have heard this as 'cars were parked all along the street', because initial /stv – / is not allowed in the rules of English, and the context strongly suggests another interpretation.

Similarly, production errors (either deliberate or accidental) in grammar — as long as they are not so gross as to be obvious — are often 'ignored' by listeners: that is to say, reanalyzed and so 'heard' as the correct form. For example, presented with the utterance 'the man are here', many listeners will use their internal knowledge of English grammar to reinterpret this, and 'hear' it as 'the men are here' (less likely would be the reinterpretation as 'the man is here').

On the phonetic level much experimental work has been done to look at how much acoustic information (in the way of formant transitions, length, etc.) is necessary for the correct identification of particular speech sounds, and some of this is reported in Chapter 28. Nevertheless, the discussion in this section allows us to address the questions raised earlier by concluding that an identical match between input and template is not required, and that the template must be flexible enough to cope with a range of phonetically differing inputs (that must still be 'similar' in a way we cannot specify here).

Phonetic and phonemic listening

As we saw in the previous section, our stored 'template' for a word or a sound does not need to have a comprehensive picture of the acoustic make-up of the input. Indeed, basic examination of naive speakers (i.e. non-phonetically trained listeners) tells us that not only do our templates not need such a complete picture, they actually lack acoustic information that is quite easy for us to find experimentally. The reason for this is that we normally listen linguistically not phonetically. By this distinction I mean that when we listen we need only be concerned with the amount of acoustic information that separates one contrastive unit of sound (or 'phoneme') from another in our language; other aspects of the sound unit will be present, but if not linguistically important will be ignored, and so not 'heard' (in reality, perceived but not comprehended).

Let us take a classic example from the English of most accents. Most naive listeners will tell you that the 'l' in 'leaf' and that in 'feel' are the same sound: they do not hear a difference between them. However, if we listen carefully, we can distinguish between them: the 'l' in 'leaf' is 'clear' ([l], usually slight palatalization, or no secondary articulation, see Chapter 10), whereas that in 'feel' is 'dark' ([ɫ], velarized). Who is right, the naive listener or the phonetician? Of course, both are. Normally, we listen phonemically, that is to say we ignore the slight differences between varieties (or 'allophones') of a phoneme. These differences are phonetic 'accidents' and do not contribute in any straightforward way to the comprehension of the message. However, it is possible to be trained to listen phonetically. In doing this the listener must divorce the acoustic signal from the semantic content as much as possible to distinguish as many shades of sound as feasible. You must listen to your native language as if it were a foreign one which you do not know.

This skill — phonetic listening — is an important one for phoneticians, and in particular for clinical phoneticians and speech pathologists. Researchers have pointed out the dangers of phonemic listening in the transcription of speech disorders in patients. Unless we have as precise a record as possible of a patient's speech output, wrong diagnoses can be made and inappropriate intervention undertaken. It is for this reason that this book uses (and introduces through Part I) the specialist phonetic symbols of the IPA and PRDS (see also the Appendices).

The conditioning of a comprehension process by phonemic listening also has an effect on second language learning. Because normally we listen in terms of the phonemes of our own language, we may find it difficult to hear phonemic distinctions in other languages that are absent in our own, or to cope with allophonic groupings in the foreign language that are phonemic in our own. For example, most dialects of Arabic lack the contrast /p/ – /b/ found in English. Not only will Arabic learners of English use [b] for target /p/, but those lacking instruction in English are likely to 'hear' English /p/ and /b/ as Arabic /b/.

In Spanish there are two sounds (or 'phones') [d] and [ð], similar to the English phones [d] and [ð]. In Spanish the two sounds are allophones (varieties) of one phoneme ([d] word initial, [ð] elsewhere), whereas in English they are separate phonemes. Many Spanish learners of English find it difficult to hear English /d/ and /ð/ as distinct, while English speakers cannot understand how this difficulty can exist! Both these features are caused by phonemic listening habits in the native languages.

Finally we can look at the English learner of French. Here we encounter the French phoneme /p/, whose chief variant is [p⁼]. The chief variant of the English /p/ is [pʰ] (see Chapter 8 for details on these differences). Not only do learners substitute [pʰ] for [p⁼], but they will hear French [p⁼] as English [pʰ], or rather they will not hear any differences between the two.

Our comprehension process, then, is informed by a lot more than the neural impulses arriving at the auditory projection area of the brain, but contributing to the process is our knowledge of the phonology, grammar and semantics of our language, and our knowledge of the world.

Further reading

The area we have been investigating here has been the subject of numerous theoretical accounts. Many of the resultant models of speech production and perception are highly complicated, however. A way into this area is provided by Dew and Jensen (1977), chapter 10, though parts of chapter 6 of Denes and Pinson (1973) may also be of help.

CHAPTER 26

Deafness

Just as in Part I of this book where we followed each discussion of aspects of articulatory phonetics with a description of how these could be impaired, so we can follow our account of hearing in Chapters 23–25 with a look at disorders of hearing, commonly termed deafness. We have seen also that hearing involves three related processes: the physical process of the peripheral auditory system, the perceptual process of the internal auditory system, and the comprehension process in the brain. The term 'deafness' has been used to cover impairments to all three of these processes (though perhaps less usually to the third of them), and in this chapter we will consider all three in turn.

We have entitled this chapter 'deafness', though in reality we will also be discussing conditions that do not always bring about a total lack of hearing. For this reason some authorities prefer the term 'hearing loss' which can encompass a whole range of hearing abilities. We will describe the methods used to measure hearing ability in Chapter 27.

Conductive deafness

Conductive deafness is the term given to any form of hearing loss originating in the peripheral auditory system, i.e. the outer ear and the middle ear, though excluding the inner ear. The term arises because problems in these areas prevent or reduce the conduction of the speech signal from the outer area to the important inner ear.

Conductive deafness is often the result of congenital disorders. These can take the form of the lack of the pinna and/or meatus. In such cases some hearing is still possible, and the lack of meatus can be rectified through surgery. Other congenital effects are loss or damage to the ear-drum and/or the ossicles of the middle ear. These too can be put right surgically.

There are various diseases of the middle ear that can cause conductive deafness. One such is otosclerosis, and is mainly found in young children. Here soft bone material grows in the middle ear cementing the ossicles to the oval window and preventing their movement. Serous otitis media ('glue ear') is a condition where pus fills the middle ear, again causing hearing loss. Suppurative otitis media is a similar condition caused by an infection of the lining of the middle ear.

The effect of conductive hearing loss is usually simply that sounds have to be louder to be heard. In most cases sounds of 50 dB or more can be heard, though the effect of otosclerosis is greater. Further, there is usually little distortion, and a hearing aid that boosts sound levels can often overcome much of the loss of hearing. As noted previously, surgery or other forms of treatment can overcome many of the causes of conductive deafness.

Sensorineural deafness

Sensorineural deafness is loss of hearing caused by impairments in the inner ear and/or auditory nerve. This type of deafness is also termed 'neural' or 'nerve' deafness, and showing the link with the aspect of hearing involved, 'perceptive' deafness. We can subdivide this category according to where the impairment occurs. Sensory, or cochlear, deafness, as the name suggests, is hearing loss attributable to damage in the cochlea; whereas neural deafness (less common than sensory) is due to nerve disease, most commonly connected with a tumour.

An example of sensory deafness might be 'high-tone deafness' where the patient is unable to, or has difficulty in responding to high frequencies. This is the result of damage to the receptor cells in the organ of Corti which deal with these frequencies. Ménière's disease is an example of neural deafness, and occurs with other symptoms including *tinnitus*. Tinnitus is the term given to the various buzzing, hissing and ringing noises that are sometimes heard in the ear which lack an external acoustic source. In Ménière's disease they occur in acute form, and are extremely distressing for the patient.

It is of course important in assessing patients with hearing loss to distinguish conductive from sensorineural deafness. We will be saying more about audiometry in the next chapter, but we can note here the main way of telling them apart. If a patient can hear sounds through the skull (i.e. by bone conduction) but not through the air, then the likelihood is that the problem is conductive hearing loss. If these two modes of conduction produce similar responses, then sensorineural loss is to be suspected.

An added difficulty in making such judgments is that mixed types can occur. This is especially so with hearing loss in the elderly, known as *presbycusis*. In this condition it is usually found that sufferers report that sounds appear fainter, as in conductive deafness. However, normally they report also that high frequency sounds are especially difficult to hear, as in some sensorineural forms of deafness. This means that hearing aids or other ways of increasing the intensity of the incoming acoustic signal (such as shouting!) will often not be the total solution. The elderly really need extra time to interpret a message: to fill in the missing or difficult sounds from the context of the utterance. Unfortunately, this extra time is often treated as lack of intelligence or a sign of senility.

Central deafness

This type of hearing loss is also termed 'cortical deafness', and is caused by damage to the auditory nerve in the brain-stem or in the auditory projection area of the cortex. In terms of our classification of hearing, this form of deafness affects comprehension, and diagnosis must take this into account. Sufferers of central deafness seem to display normal ear usage when tested with pure tone audiometry (see Chapter 27), but speech audiometry will show that the ability to understand speech is impaired. Patients with this condition appear unable to interpret speech sounds and integrate them into an appreciation of the linguistic content of the acoustic signal.

The difficulty with any diagnosis of central deafness is to ascertain whether the impairment is restricted to an audiological form, or whether the problem in comprehension is in fact part of a wider language disability affecting both speech production and perception. Such problems are found in, for example, Wernicke's aphasia and childhood autism.

Unlike conductive deafness where treatment can often produce amelioration of the condition, central deafness is like many types of sensorineural deafness in being not normally reversible.

The onset of deafness

While it is important to look at deafness in terms of what aspect of hearing is impaired, it is also useful from a linguistic point of view to examine the stage at which deafness came about. The distinction we work with here is between congenital and acquired hearing loss.

Congenital deafness (which, like acquired, can occur with conductive, sensorineural, or central types of hearing loss) means that the disorder was present at birth. It might be that the disorder has a genetic origin, as in some of the cases of conductive deafness discussed above. Alternatively it could come about due to birth difficulties or disease or injury affecting the foetus before birth. Acquired deafness, of course, refers to hearing loss due to disease or injury received throughout childhood or adulthood, and we have previously discussed the hearing loss associated with aging.

Congenital deafness, and acquired deafness in young children before they have learnt to speak, present particular problems from the language point of view. The way hearing children learn language is, of course, primarily through matching a heard stimulus with an object or situation, at least in the early stages. This sort of procedure is not available to the prelinguistic profoundly deaf child, leading to the situation of being both deaf and dumb. However, deafness does not of itself mean that someone is unable to speak. With intensive teaching this type of deaf child can be taught to produce speech, though often this is limited in its range and comprehensibility. Because of this, alternative communication strategies are used both to 'speak' to deaf people, and for them to use to communicate with others. These systems take various forms, but most are 'signing systems' of some kind.

Signing systems can be of numerous types. Some rely on a knowledge of spelling as the signs represent letters of the alphabet, as in Figure 26.1, while others are 'sign languages' where words and meanings are constructed out of signs. Examples of these latter are American Sign Language, British Sign Language, and

Figure 26.1a Finger spelling: American one-handed and British two-handed systems

American Manual Alphabet

(Signs shown as they appear to the person reading them.)

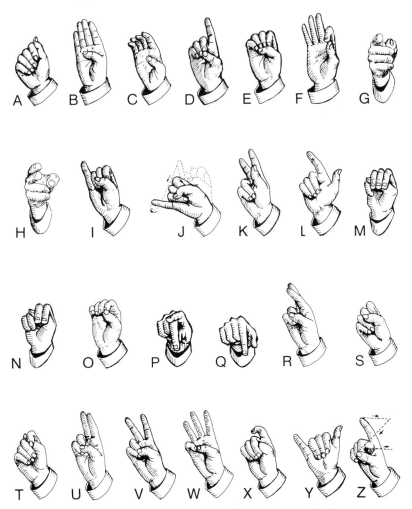

Gallaudet University Press. Reprinted by permission.

Figure 26.1b

The Royal National Institute for the Deaf

STANDARD MANUAL ALPHABET

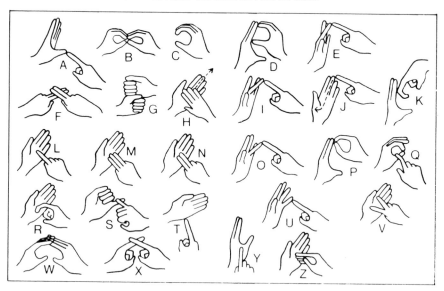

the Paget–Gorman Sign System (see Figure 26.2). Cued Speech augments lip-reading abilities which many deaf people learn, by the speaker using various hand shapes to cue particular phonological contrasts during speech. This is illustrated in Figure 26.3.

There is controversy amongst teachers of the deaf as to whether sign systems should be taught as well as (or instead of) attempts to introduce actual speech. We have not got the space here to follow this, sometimes bitter, debate, but Crystal (1980, pp. 135f) can be consulted for further information.

Deafness that is acquired postlinguistically (that is to say after language has developed) has different consequences. While the profoundly deaf of this category may still need to develop a new strategy for comprehension of others (e.g. lip-reading), they retain the ability to produce speech. However, the speech of this group of the hearing-impaired is often marked by disturbances to the prosodic (or suprasegmental) aspects. Intonation is often 'flattened', with loudness and tempo often uncontrolled. Certain individual speech sounds may also be affected. It would appear that many of these problems are due to the fact that such speakers are no longer able to monitor their own speech production auditorily, and so cannot correct errors in these fields. The area of feedback in speech is returned to in Chapter 29.

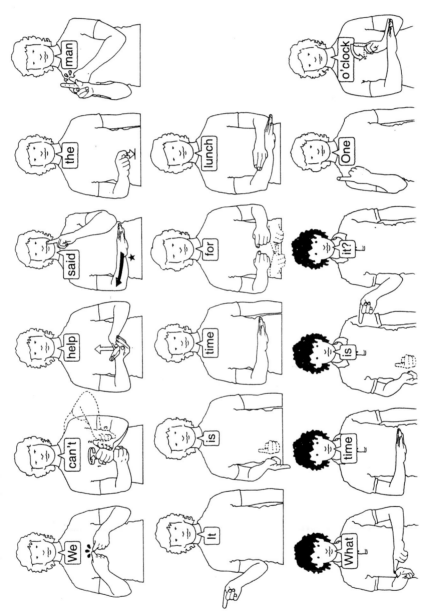

Figure 26.2 The Paget-Gorman Sign System

Figure 26.3 Cued speech

Cued Speech for speakers of Standard Southern British pronunciation

(The sounds are written in Dr. R. Orin Cornett's 'Fuhnetik Speling')

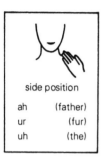

side position	
ah	(father)
ur	(fur)
uh	(the)

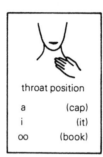

throat position	
a	(cap)
i	(it)
oo	(book)

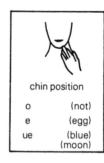

chin position	
o	(not)
e	(egg)
ue	(blue) (moon)

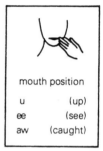

mouth position	
u	(up)
ee	(see)
aw	(caught)

Diphthongs are cued as glides of the hand between the appropriate positions; e.g. ie from ah to i and ou from ah to oo

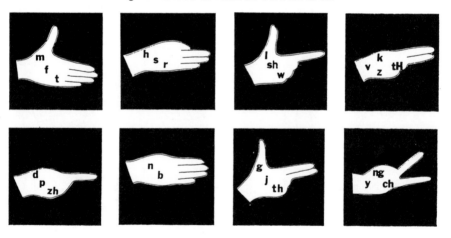

The hand-shape shown in Figure 1 is also used with an isolated vowel — that is a vowel not preceded by a consonant.

Teachers of the deaf have generally been concerned with providing communication systems for the prelinguistic deaf (often in cooperation with speech pathologists). However, the postlinguistic deaf patient is usually the responsibility of the speech pathologist in terms of the rehabilitation of communication. Various techniques have been used with such patients to improve, or reestablish, their speech abilities. For example, the electrolaryngograph (see Chapter 12) is particularly useful in correcting problems with intonation.

Further reading

A brief introduction to the study of deafness is given in Crystal (1980, pp. 129f). However, there are many other good texts, amongst which we can name Meadow (1980) for deafness in children, and Ballantyne (1977) for a more general approach. Wolff (1973) also provides an easy introduction to hearing and language, and includes discussion of various signing systems. References to audiology are included in the next chapter.

CHAPTER 27

Audiological Measurement

In the previous chapter we noted that hearing loss could occur to different degrees in different patients. This implies that we can measure hearing ability, and in particular our response to different degrees of loudness (often termed 'hearing acuity'). As explored in Chapter 28, there are numerous psychoacoustic techniques which allow us to measure subjects' responses to many different aspects of speech perception, but in investigating hearing acuity and hearing loss there have been developed certain techniques that are relatively straightforward to undertake and produce reliable results for the clinician.

Procedures of this kind are part of the area of study termed 'audiology' (i.e. the science of hearing). Audiological measurement, also known as audiometry, is a very important aspect in the diagnosis of extent and type of hearing loss, and is an essential preliminary to the planning of remediation by the speech pathologist or other interested professionals.

In this chapter we will discuss some of the different approaches to audiometry, and the sort of results we get with different categories of deaf patient. It is not intended, however, to serve in any way as a guide to undertaking audiological measurement, for which appropriate training from qualified teachers must be given.

Pure tone audiometry

Pure tone audiometry is probably the easiest audiometric technique to undertake, though we will see below that it is perhaps not the most appropriate from the point of view of speech. The technique involves presenting to the subject a series of artificially produced pure tones, that is to say tones consisting of only one frequency, though a range of frequencies is used in each test. The tones are presented to one ear at a time so the audiologist can determine whether any hearing loss is equally or differentially present in both ears. The mode of presentation can be altered, in that air conduction can be used by having the subject wear headphones through which the signal is fed, or bone conduction can be chosen and the signal applied to the bone behind the ear. Whichever form of presentation is chosen, the required response of subjects is the same: they are asked to indicate when they are able to hear the particular tone being presented. Therefore, the audiologist alters the intensity of the signal from a point of loudness just below where normal hearing people would hear the tone, and increases the loudness gradually until it becomes just audible to the subject. This 'threshold level' is then marked on a special form called an audiogram and is measured in dB above the 'normal' threshold level for that particular pure tone frequency.

As noted in the previous chapter, pure tone audiometry is a useful diagnostic tool for distinguishing examples of conductive deafness from sensorineural (providing the patient does not demonstrate mixed type). Figure 27.1 shows how this difference can be seen audiometrically. The first audiogram shows a general lowering of thresholds by about the same amount right across the frequency spectrum. On the other hand, the second shows a greater lowering of threshold levels in the higher frequencies, as is often found in sensorineural hearing loss.

There are, however, some disadvantages in the use of pure tone audiometry with the hearing impaired. It is not really appropriate to apply the results of this technique directly to the assessment of patients' abilities to hear speech. There are several reasons for this: firstly the stimuli being used are acoustically fairly unlike the normal speech signal which is considerably more complex. Secondly, the test is recording when the subject can just hear the tone, so it does not tell us what level the patient needs for the sound to be 'useful', i.e. if it were a speech sound, when it could be regularly distinguished in conversation. It might seem that we could have an overall figure by which to increase the threshold to reach this level; along the lines of 'if it can be regularly heard at x dB, then it can be regularly perceived at x + y dB'. However, this is not the case. Different people react in different ways to the increase of the intensity of a signal: for some there is a concomitant regular increase in loudness, for others there may be a great jump in loudness (termed 'recruitment'), and for others still there is little perceived increase in loudness.

A third problem involves background noise. In speech we are always encountering various degrees of background noise: traffic noise in the street, hiss on a telephone line, other conversations in the workplace, and so on. This, however, can be reflected to some extent in pure tone audiometry by using masking, i.e. the addition of random noise across the frequency range (sometimes termed 'white noise'). Audiograms, consequently, allow you to show whether a masked or an unmasked signal was used.

A final problem we need to consider is the accuracy of the patients' responses. It is recognized that some patients are going to be more careful in indicating the threshold of hearing than others; in other words they will indicate a loudness level higher than others. It is usually accepted, therefore, that most audiograms are only reliable within a range of 5–10dB either side of the indicated threshold. This may be greater in certain cases of neural deafness, where tinnitus and other forms of internal background noise may hamper the subject's accuracy in reporting

Figure 27.1 Pure tone audiograms of two types of hearing loss: (i) conductive, (ii) sensorineural

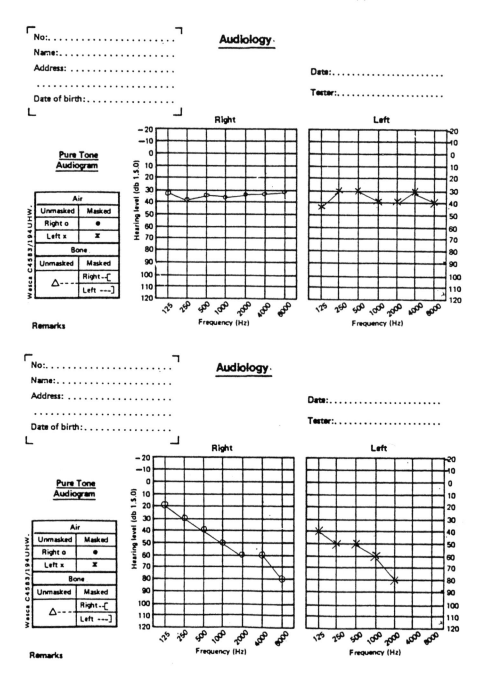

threshold levels. Nevertheless, despite this limitation on total accuracy, the audiogram will still report overall trends of hearing ability.

We may have seemed to be overly critical of pure tone audiometry, but it has to be stressed that it is a quick and generally reliable way of diagnosing type of deafness, and general hearing ability. If, however, we want to obtain more speech-related information we may need to supplement this approach with others.

Speech audiometry

Audiological measurement using speech or sounds of various qualities as stimulus has been developed as an alternative or addition to pure tone audiometry. As the name suggests, this technique uses speech, in particular lists of words or phrases specially devised to contain a balance of the sounds of the language in question. The stimuli can be presented to the subject live, or via a tape recording, but if live then the tester should not be visible to the subject to avoid the cues that would be available to those who have learnt lip-reading. The subject is required to respond by repeating the stimulus to the tester, or sometimes by indicating the correct version from a set of similar answers on paper.

Audiograms for this technique are organized differently. The loudness level of the stimulus in dB is still shown. The tester still controls the intensity of the speech signal, but the other scale of measurement is the percentage of correct responses at the different dB levels. Depending upon what aspect of speech is being investigated, speech audiograms can be scored in terms of percentage correct phrases, words or phonemes.

Figure 27.2 shows a composite speech audiogram from three different subjects. The left hand curve is the typical result for a normal hearing subject. It shows that only a small percentage of items are correct below 10 dB, rising to about half at 20 dB, and 100 per cent at about 35–40 dB. The middle curve is similar in shape to

Figure 27.2 Speech audiograms

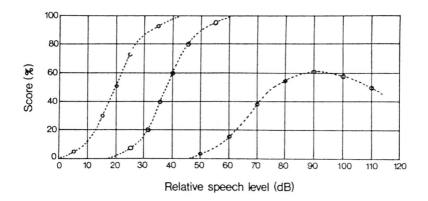

the first, but on average each stage seems to require an increase of some 20dB (in this example) in the signal intensity. This is the typical response curve of someone suffering conductive hearing loss, and as noted in the previous chapter, speech can be made intelligible if loudness is increased sufficiently. The final curve is typical of sensorineural deafness. As with the other two examples, the curve at first shows an increase in loudness. However, at a certain point (here, 90 dB) the score rises no higher, and any increase in loudness actually causes a decrease in intelligibility: 100 per cent correct is never reached. This pattern reflects the kind of damage encountered in sensorineural hearing loss, namely inner ear impairment: amplifying the signal not only increases the loudness, but also the distortion caused by the inner ear problem.

There are also problems encountered in speech audiometry. The most important of these is the fact that very young children and other prelinguistically deaf subjects will naturally be unable to respond to stimuli in the required way. It may be possible to attempt identification tasks involving nonsense syllables, but even this may be difficult to explain, and will not be very satisfactory.

Conclusion

Although audiological measurement of various types can give us a fairly good guide to the hearing acuity of some deaf patients, it does have limitations, especially with children. Nevertheless, work with children has shown that there is a correlation between audiometric results and the likelihood of the child being able to develop language. The classification of hearing loss has been attempted, derived from average scores in dB taken from pure tone audiometry. These can be shown as follows:

25–40 dB loss:	slight	
40–60dB loss:	moderate	partially hearing
60–85dB loss:	severe	
85/90dB + loss:	profound	

The partially hearing group may all develop language to some extent, though the moderate and severe groups will need hearing aids. However, the profoundly deaf group are unlikely to develop language without special education. Audiometry, therefore, is an important diagnostic tool for children, but also for adults. As we noted in Chapter 26, appropriate remediation must depend upon the diagnosis of the patients into the various types of deafness.

Further reading

A good introduction to audiology is found in Martin (1981), whereas audiological measurement is described in Katz (1985) and Beagley (1981). A recent survey of speech audiometry is found in Martin (1987).

CHAPTER 28

Psychoacoustic Experiments

In Chapter 24 we looked at the perception of sound and outlined some of the features of sound signals that humans can perceive. However, we only know what these are through experimentation that combines the acoustic study of the sound signal with the psychological testing of subjects' responses: hence psychoacoustics. Naturally, this area of study cannot be an exact science, as we have to rely on subjects' self-reporting (albeit in a controlled fashion). Nevertheless, results across subjects show a remarkable degree of consistency, to an extent that we can be sure that our results are relatively accurate.

We reported in Chapter 24 some of the results of psychoacoustic experimentation; in particular, aspects of perception to do with frequency and intensity, or in perceptual terms, pitch and loudness. In this chapter we will describe some of the experimental procedures, and then those results connected with the perception of specific sounds, or groups of speech sounds.

Experimental procedures

When considering what procedures can be used in perceptual experiments we must not only discuss the sort of stimulus used, but also the choice of subjects. Unless one is particularly interested in the reactions of trained linguists and phoneticians, the psychoacoustic experimenter usually chooses what we call the 'naive listener'. This is, of course, not a pejorative term, but means that the subject concerned has no especial training in phonetics. It can be argued also, that those trained in a foreign language have also learnt to listen in a different way (see Chapter 25) and will not be representative of the naive listener. Bilinguals may also have developed a listening skill different from the monoglot, and so such subjects may have to be considered separately. Other variables to be considered include the age and sex of the subjects.

The choice of stimulus presented to the subjects depends, naturally, on the precise area of perception being investigated. This may be to do with distinguishing one sound from a closely similar one, or making judgments to do with loudness, pitch or rhythm. Whatever the precise area of speech being examined, there are four basic types of questions that can be asked in these experiments: detection, discrimination, identification, and scaling.

As the term suggests, *detection* exercises involve the subject in determining the point when the stimulus becomes detectable. Naturally, this type of test is connected with loudness studies. *Discrimination* studies look at just noticeable differences (see Chapter 24) between stimuli, whether this is in terms of loudness, pitch or differences between individual speech sounds (often vowel sounds). *Identification* tasks involve asking a subject to classify a stimulus according to a set of labels normally provided by the tester (often a forced choice between two). This sort of work is often found in studies of individual consonant sounds, and we will return to this later. *Scaling* studies involve the subject in placing a stimulus onto a scale of values (either numerical or intensive). Several such scales to do with loudness and pitch were described in Chapter 24.

The ways in which the stimulus is presented also differ from study to study. In brief, 'adjustment' presentations involve the subject in making continuous adjustments to the stimulus, often until a fixed point is reached. In 'limits' presentations the change in values of the stimulus is controlled by the experimenter in fixed steps. Finally, 'constant stimuli' tests utilize a set of randomly presented stimuli to which the subject must respond by, perhaps, identifying one of them.

Finally, and perhaps most importantly, we must look at what kind of acoustic signal is to be utilized in these experiments. For some experiments natural speech is perfectly sufficient. Sometimes this is recorded in sound-proof conditions to give the best possible signal, but sometimes the recordings involve 'masking' (by adding noise of various frequencies) to mimic the sort of background noise we often encounter in normal conversation. By using masking we can discover just when speech becomes impossible to hear.

However, when we are interested in looking at individual sounds, and the acoustic cues which help us to discriminate between similar sounds, we often need to use synthetic speech rather than natural. By using synthetic speech we can be sure to avoid the variation inherent in natural speech because, of course, in scientific experimentation we need to control variation and keep everything constant except the feature under investigation — and only with synthetic speech is this possible. Further, using synthetic speech allows us easily to alter the acoustic signal in such a way that enables us to discover which aspects of the signal are important in perception and which not.

Acoustic cues in speech perception

From experiments mainly with synthetic speech phoneticians have been able to discover the main acoustic cues in speech (Fry, 1976, contains details of some of these experiments, while Fry, 1979, summarizes them). In this section we will attempt to look at some of these.

Acoustic cues for vowels

The main acoustic cues for vowel recognition is the relationship between the first and second formant (F1 and F2, see Chapter 18). Of course, these values are not fixed for every speaker, and children, for example, will have F1 and F2 at higher frequencies than adults. Nevertheless, listeners can easily adjust to such range differences and it is the relationship between the formants that is the cue we need for distinguishing between most vowels.

Other acoustic features also have a part to play. To some extent for English, but more so in many other languages, the duration of the vowel segment allows us to tell apart two vowels that in other respects may be very similar. Differences in intensity may also be of help in telling high vowels from low, especially when there is masking of the speech signal. Nevertheless, such differences are not great (about 7dB).

Acoustic cues for phonation differences

Here we will examine only the voiced–voiceless contrast, as it is the most important phonatory distinction linguistically. For languages where this distinction is literally the presence versus absence of vocal cord vibration (and for English in intervocalic position) the acoustic cue for voiced sounds is the presence of low-frequency energy and a periodic sound wave tied to the larynx frequency. However, other features are also present for this distinction in many languages. For example, in English initial stop consonants, other cues are present. The most important of these is voice-onset time (VOT). This is not simply a durational cue, despite the name, but is connected to the presence versus absence of aspiration (see Chapter 8). If an initial plosive release is followed by a relatively long VOT there results a period of time during which only voiceless 'noise' is heard (i.e. aspiration), and this serves as a cue for voiceless sounds. If the VOT is short, such aspiration is missing giving us the cue for voice.

Duration of the vowel and consonant segments is also an important perceptual cue for final consonants in English. A long vowel followed by a short consonant is the cue for a 'voiced' consonant, whereas the opposite tells us it is 'voiceless'. Finally, intensity is usually greater for voiceless sounds than voiced, as is suggested by the terms 'fortis' and 'lenis' often used as well as voiceless–voiced.

Acoustic cues for manner of articulation

The cue for plosives and affricates is the presence of an interruption in the speech signal lasting from about 40–120 msec. Affricates are further distinguished by the presence of a noise component, and this cue by itself marks out fricative sounds. The noise component may last from 70–140msec.

The other main manner types (nasals, laterals and semi-vowels) lack these two cues, having instead the presence of a continuous tone (i.e. voice). The cue for nasals is a low frequency resonance and then the absence of energy above this and below 2000Hz (see Chapter 19). Both laterals and semivowels are cued by vowel-like formants, with duration of the formant transitions telling them apart: these being faster for the laterals.

Acoustic cues for place of articulation

The major cue for place of articulation is given by the formant transitions from vowel to consonant or vice versa, particularly the transitions of the F2 of the vowel (see initial discussion of this in Chapter 22). Experimentation with synthetic speech has shown that when the F2 transition has a minus value (i.e. when the movement, dependent upon position in the syllable, is either towards or away from a frequency lower than that which would be normal in the vowel in isolation) then the place signalled is bilabial. If the F2 transition has a plus value (the movement towards or away from a frequency higher than 'normal') then a velar place is signalled. Alveolar place is signalled by either a very slight plus or minus transition.

Also working as a cue for place (especially for fricatives and aspirates) is noise filtering. The difference in noise range for these sounds was noted in Chapter 20, and it is a recognition of these that allows the discrimination of /θ/, /s/ and /ʃ/, and so on.

Conclusion

The acoustic cues we have investigated here have been confined to individual segments. We also, of course, have to recognize many rhythmic aspects of speech such as stress and intonation. The cues for these are mainly to do with our discrimination of larynx activity, which also conveys much information on voice quality. We do not have the space here to follow up these matters, but we have been able to explore the major cues for speech recognition.

Naturally, any impairment to the ability to perceive aspects of these cues (see Chapter 26) will lead to a selective inability to contrast speech sounds, and the gradual breakdown of the comprehension of a phonological system. Being aware of what cues signal what distinctions enables the speech pathologist or audiologist to see more easily how comprehension is being affected and to plan appropriate intervention.

Further reading

Fry (1979) goes into a lot of detail on the acoustic cues for the recognition of English vowels and consonants (chapter 11), though similar details can be found in other phonetics texts referred to in this book. Fry does not, however, go into a great deal of information about methods of psychoacoustics, which are described in some detail in Richards (1976). Other sources of information are Denes and Pinson (1973) chapter 8, and papers in Lehiste (1967) and Fry (1976).

CHAPTER 29

Feedback in Speech

We have already seen that feedback plays an important role in speech when we looked at the effect deafness has on peoples' speech production (Chapter 26). Here, the loss of the ability to hear your own speech means you are not able to monitor your production as well as hearing people can. This is what we mean by the term 'feedback': the monitoring of your speech. As in any human activity, speech has to be continually monitored to make sure it is not going wrong, and to correct it when it does. However many times we use a hammer to hit a nail, this activity is not automatic, it needs monitoring. It sometimes does go wrong, and we hit our thumbs by mistake, but then we make adjustments, and then only the very unlucky (or clumsy!) would hit their thumb twice in succession; but imagine undertaking this task with no 'feedback' — say with a blindfold on — the chances are we would end up with a very bruised hand!

In the same way, speech minus feedback will usually result in a progressive degeneration of accuracy, thus badly affecting comprehension. We have already noted that hearing is one of the feedback mechanisms, and it is for this reason that the topic has been included in the part of the book dealing with auditory phonetics. However, auditory feedback is just one type that we know about, and the examination of feedback in speech in reality belongs to the study of the complete model of speech production and perception. In discussing feedback in the following sections, therefore, we will be using a very basic speech production model, but it must be stressed that this is only rudimentary and will not include all that we currently know about the process.

A Model of speech production

Following usual practice we can attempt a simple model of speech production diagrammatically as in Figure 29.1. As is normally done, this diagram utilizes a series of boxes, standing for the various operations undertaken in speaking, linked by lines which show the relationship between these operations. Figure 29.1 is based on

Figure 29.1 A model of speech production

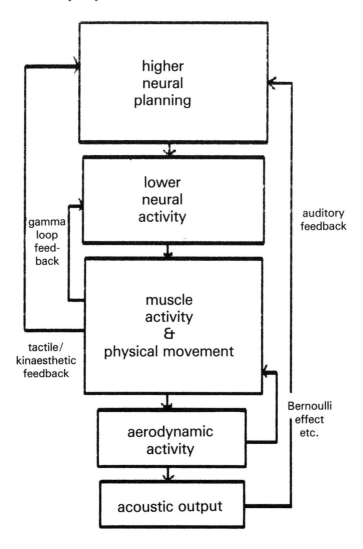

Netsell (1973), which although a relatively early work, is sufficient for our purposes here as an introduction to the topic. Even so, various modifications have been made to the original.

Our first box, called here 'higher neural planning', really collapses several processes into one (discussion of which can be found in Code and Ball, 1988). Under this title we are subsuming the brain activity responsible for devising a message, organizing it into the phonological units necessary for speech, and planning and ordering the necessary nerve impulses to produce the final phonetic effect. The second box is labelled 'lower neural activity', and this covers the actual nerve impulses as they travel to the muscles along the neural pathways. The third box, 'muscle activity and physical movement', is another composite. It covers the muscular events triggered by the neural impulses and the resultant movement of the vocal organs. Resulting from many of the actions of box 3 is 'aerodynamic activity', and this is box 4. Features such as initiation and air stream mechanisms (see Chapter 2) are covered here. The final box, 'the acoustic output', is the result of interaction between air flows and physical movements in the vocal tract.

The diagram also demonstrates feedback. Some of this is automatic, such as the link between box 3 and 4. An example of this linkage might be the Bernoulli effect, where in voiced phonation the movement of the air between the vocal cords actually is responsible to a large degree for the sucking in of the vocal cords.

The other feedback lines all go to higher, neural, levels, which must naturally be the case if feedback is to be of any help in the control and correction of the speech signal. These three feedback systems are the auditory feedback system, the tactile/kinaesthetic feedback system and the gamma-loop feedback system, and they will be considered in turn.

Auditory feedback

Chapter 26 pointed out the importance of auditory feedback to the maintenance of an accurate phonetic output. However, in terms of speech monitoring, auditory feedback is in fact limited. The reason for this is the time it takes for the information to return to the higher neural planning stage. Figure 29.1, although crude, clearly shows this feedback system is the longest.

By 'longest' we are of course being relative. The time it takes from the movement of a speaker's articulators until he hears the resultant sound and can make any necessary alterations to the articulator movements is between about 160 and 250 msec. This is naturally a very short time, but in terms of speech production this may well be longer than many individual segments. So, for example, stop consonants will usually be over before the speaker can perceive them auditorily, and therefore correction will be impossible. Longer sounds (some vowels and some fricatives for example) may be able to be monitored using this system, nevertheless a considerable amount of the segment may be uttered before any intervention can take place.

In utterances of any length, however, auditory feedback is very useful for monitoring non-segmental prosodic features such as loudness, pitch, stress and rate of articulation. As it is often just these very features that are affected in the deaf, this would appear to support the view that it is this feedback system that is primarily responsible for monitoring suprasegmental speech aspects.

Tactile/kinaesthetic feedback

Under this head is included a series of linked receptors that are found throughout the vocal tract. Tactile receptors are responsible for information about touch and pressure; kinaesthetic receptors tell us about movement and the physical positions of the vocal organs. These receptors, therefore, provide the speaker with information about the execution of the neural commands of speech, about the accuracy of the movement and placing of the different articulators.

Different articulators have differing kinds and numbers of these tactile/kinaesthetic receptors. The tongue has many of these receptors, and therefore we can accurately monitor both tongue position (important for place of articulation) and pressure (important for manner of articulation). On the other hand, the palate does not have many such receptors. For speech this lack is not important, because when the palate is the passive articulator the tongue will be the active one, and so accuracy can be monitored via the latter.

We know that tactile/kinaesthetic feedback is an important monitoring system from several pieces of evidence. Individuals who have an impairment in their receptors (sometimes this is congenital) demonstrate articulation disorders. Also, we can mimic this loss experimentally through the use of local anaesthetics, and studies of this sort have also produced articulation errors.

Figure 29.1 clearly shows that tactile/kinaesthetic feedback has a shorter route than auditory feedback, that is to say it is quicker. Nevertheless, it is reckoned that such feedback is still too slow to monitor some of the fine muscle activity necessary for certain speech sounds. To account for these, an even shorter time span is needed.

Gamma-loop feedback

Not so much is known about this system than the previous two; however, there is evidence to suggest that a fast, 'low-level' feedback does exist to monitor the fine control of articulator movement needed for speech. As shown in Figure 29.1, the system involves a link between muscle activity and the lower neural activity level. This implies that this form of monitoring is a quasi-automatic system, and unlike the previous two types does not involve brain activity.

The theory behind gamma-loop (or 'proprioceptive') feedback is based on the physiology of the neuromuscular system. Simplifying this system considerably, we can state that neural impulses originating at higher levels of planning are transmitted via alpha and gamma motor neurons to the muscles. The resultant movements in the muscle are sensed in what is termed the 'muscle spindle' and impulses are sent back from these spindles via the gamma system to impinge on the alpha motor neurons again.

We can reasonably conclude from this system that gamma motor neurons can modify the alpha signals in some way to provide the fine motor control we need in speech. The returning signal via the gamma neurons must be subjected to an automatic 'comparison' process with the intended outgoing signal, and changes made to any deviations.

Conclusion

Speech is a highly complex process with accuracy of control needed in very short time units. As with most human activities, a monitoring system is required to ensure that accuracy is maintained. As we have seen, some aspects of speech are amenable to a monitoring system based on auditory feedback; however, other aspects need faster feedback such as is found in tactile/kinaesthetic and gamma-loop feedback. Impairment to any of these systems will lead to distortion of different aspects of speech output. Intervention to overcome the loss of auditory feedback can be quite successful (see Chapter 26); however, damage to the other systems is more difficult to deal with. Nevertheless, a procedure has been developed by speech scientists to explore and improve tactile abilities in speakers. This is termed 'oral stereognosis', and consists of exercising the patient's oral tactile receptors by getting them to describe the shape of small unseen objects inserted into the mouth.

Feedback, then, is just as important a part of the speech production process as is the movement of articulators or the creation of air flows. Impairment to feedback can be just as disruptive to communication as impairment to articulation, and needs as much attention paid to it by the speech pathologist.

Further reading

The Netsell (1973) work referred to above is recommended for further reading, together with Code and Ball (1988), although the latter requires some knowledge of the various acquired neurological disorders of speech (aphasia, dysarthria and apraxia of speech). Many other texts do mention feedback systems in speech, but the introductory texts, as a rule, do not attempt to construct models in the way done here. Borden and Harris (1980) have a good discussion on feedback in speech.

CHAPTER 30

Delayed Auditory Feedback

This and the following two chapters look at a set of auditory techniques that have been used for research into speech pathology as well as phonetics in general.

The first of these is delayed auditory feedback (DAF). We saw in Chapter 29 the importance of auditory feedback in the speech production process, and we also noted the temporal aspect of all feedback systems. It is possible to alter the normal time gap involved in auditory feedback and so delay auditory feedback to a greater or lesser extent. Mechanically, this process is comparatively easy to undertake. With a good reel-to-reel tape recorder, modifications can be made to delay feedback (via headphones) by 80, 160, 330 and 660 msec. Various specialist DAF instruments have been produced, and, for example, the Aberdeen Speech Aid provides a continuous range of delay times from 30 to 300 msec.

In the remainder of this chapter we will examine both the effects of DAF and its use in clinical phonetics.

DAF and normal speakers

The effect of DAF on normal speakers is well known, and demonstrates a set of changes to normal speech patterns, both indirect and direct. The indirect changes include a reduction in speech tempo, and a raising of both intensity and frequency of the acoustic output. It would appear that these features are the result of the speakers' attempts to overcome the influence of the DAF. The direct effects are perhaps more far-reaching, and include repetition of syllables and of continuant consonants, misarticulations, omissions, substitutions and additions of segments, and deletion of word endings. In fact, these features have appeared to many researchers to be 'artificial stuttering'.

A body of research exists on DAF and normal speakers, and amongst the findings are details on the level of DAF needed to create this artificial stuttering, and correlations between such levels and the age of the speaker. This research indicates that for young children (4–6 years) the most disruptive delay time is 500 msec, while older children (6–9 years) show that 400 msec causes the most problems. With adults this time reduces still further to 200 msec, though for older adults (60 years +) the figure rises again to 400 msec.

Investigations on the normal population also have shown that there may well be a difference in response to DAF by men and women, with males more vulnerable to the process than females. These findings are somewhat tentative, however, and perhaps a more important difference is that between speakers who are generally more fluent and use a faster tempo and those who are less fluent and slower. The latter demonstrate more disruption under DAF than the former.

The main reason for undertaking DAF research on normal populations is to explore the role of auditory feedback in speech. Some researchers feel that the considerable disruption to speech under DAF conditions is a result of conflict between one form of feedback (tactile-kinaesthetic and/or gamma-loop) which gives information that all is well, and auditory feedback which states that something is wrong.

DAF and disordered speech

The DAF procedure has been used in studies of disordered as well as normal speech. Naturally, as DAF causes artificial stuttering in normal speakers, it is not surprising that the main disordered speech population with which DAF has been investigated is that of stutterers. It is interesting that, while the main effect of DAF on normal populations is to induce artificial stuttering, the main effect with stutterers is to reduce disfluency. Indeed, the more severe the fluency problem the better the improvement seen under DAF.

However, as with normal speakers, it would appear that the timing of the delay is important. Unlike the production of artificial stuttering, it would seem that these positive effects need a much shorter delay in auditory feedback, though there is with stutterers considerable variation from subject to subject. Various studies have shown that disfluent speakers generally have two critical delay times: the one that produces maximum fluency, and the one (as with normals) that produces the maximum disfluency. It seems the first is relatively short (perhaps around 50 msec on average), while the second might well be longer than that found with fluent speakers.

The precise nature of this effect with stutterers is still unclear. It might be thought that DAF, and the similar technique of 'masking' (where low-frequency noise is played via headphones to the subject), are simply distractors, enabling the stutterer to avoid auditory feedback. However, both approaches only work with particular delay times or particular frequencies of noise suggesting that something more complicated is involved. It is clear that DAF interacts in some way with both the temporal organization of the speech production process and with the auditory feedback system, but more research is needed before we learn in precisely what way.

DAF has also been studied with patients suffering from aphasia, apraxia of speech and dysarthria. Numerous studies have been undertaken in this area, many with the purpose of comparing different categories of aphasic patient under DAF conditions. It would appear that there is indeed a differential response to DAF amongst these patients. The speech of conduction aphasics may well be improved by the use of DAF at a particular delay level, whereas at the other extreme the speech of Broca's aphasics is badly affected. It is doubtful whether DAF can be used with aphasics as a remediation tool; however, it may have some value as part of a battery of assessment techniques.

Clinical application of DAF

As we have seen from the discussion in the previous section, the most likely practical application of DAF in the speech pathology clinic is with stutterers. Indeed, training programmes have been devised which utilize DAF as part of a behaviour modification approach. The behaviour to be modified is speech rate, and the aim is to reduce this to bring about a slow tempo, termed 'prolonged speech'. This is brought about through a step-by-step approach involving three main phases: establishment, transfer and maintenance. Each phase consists of numerous stages, with a criterion of five minutes fluent speech before moving on to the next stage. The procedure involves at first the establishement in the clinic of fluency in various speaking tasks (reading, conversation etc.), followed by the transfer of this to situations outside the clinic together with exercise for maintaining the fluency achieved over time.

DAF was primarily employed during the establishment phase as a way of slowing the speech rate. The delay time was initially set at 250 msec, though it was gradually brought down to 50 msec, and finally to no delay at all. This programme, taking twenty hours of therapy to complete has been successful with a wide range of stutterers.

This use of DAF, however, was primarily for its effect in slowing speech. Other researchers have pointed to its direct effect on fluency as being a possible clinical tool. For example, it can be used to show stutterers that even normal speakers will demonstrate disfluency, or conversely to demonstrate to stutterers that they can achieve fluency when subject to DAF. This may well go some way to break down the dangerous feelings many stutterers have that they are somehow 'apart' from other speakers and can never achieve fluency.

It has also been suggested that prolonged exposure to DAF allows stutterers to learn to 'beat the machine' and thereby move away from auditory feedback to rely instead on proprioceptive. This assumes, however, that an impairment to the auditory feedback system is the primary cause of stuttering, and this is by no means certain.

Finally, we can consider the long-term use of DAF equipment not as a means of 'curing' stuttering, but as a permanent 'aid' to overcoming it, in much the same form as a hearing aid. Unfortunately, preliminary studies indicate that, just as normal speakers become 'immune' to DAF after a time, it appears that stutterers, too, eventually show a diminution of the improvement to fluency initially caused by DAF.

In terms of clinical applications, DAF has not been used with many other speech problems apart from stuttering. Studies with speakers suffering from Parkinson's disease have shown that certain of these patients do benefit from a treatment programme using DAF. It would appear that improvement is found in those patients where the disease has affected aspects of fluency or tempo, other patients did not show any improvement. Long term use of DAF at 50 msec delay time resulted in one of the patients maintaining improvement, while with the other, the improvement decreased and speech patterns returned to pretreatment levels after about a year.

It would appear, then, that DAF may be useful in the treatment of all types of disfluency whatever the origin, but uncertainty as to the long-term efficacy of such treatment remains.

Conclusion

DAF is of interest to the speech pathologist from both a theoretical and practical viewpoint. A continued study of DAF effects will be able to tell us more about the nature of stuttering and of the normal speech production and feedback processes. Further, the development of small, easy-to-wear DAF devices will allow patients to continue their DAF treatment outside the clinical situation.

Further reading

Readers wanting further information on both the technique and its application should consult the relevant chapter by Code in Code and Ball (1984). This contains further, more technical, references for those who wish to explore the area further.

CHAPTER 31

Dichotic Listening

In our discussion of auditory phonetics so far in this part of the book we have assumed that the hearing process is basically a unitary one, progressing through a set of stages from the acoustic signal to the ultimate comprehension of the message. We have in effect been ignoring the fact that in normal hearing populations, hearing involves binaural processing of the input, that is to say, **two** ears are involved.

In Chapter 29 we noted that audiometry can be used with the hearing-impaired to determine if there is a difference in hearing acuity between the two ears. There has also grown up since the 1950s a body of research on differing hearing abilities of the two ears in the non-hearing impaired population. This research is not, however, in terms of acuity, but of differential abilities dependent upon the nature of the stimulus. Such studies utilize the technique known as 'dichotic listening', and extrapolating from the work on normal subjects, studies have also been undertaken with various language-disordered subjects. Dichotic listening measures ear advantages for differing stimuli, from which many researchers have inferred differences in brain behaviour between the left and right hemispheres of the brain. In this chapter we will look at the technique of dichotic listening, and some of the findings of the studies using it.

The technique of dichotic listening

Dichotic listening studies involve the presentation of auditory stimuli (linguistic or otherwise) to subjects who have to identify them, usually from a set of possible choices. What makes the technique different from other psychoacoustic recognition tasks is that each stimulus involves the simultaneous presentation of different material to each ear. In other words at the same time that the right ear receives stimulus x, the left ear receives stimulus y. Such a technique requires that the stimuli are presented from a stereo tape recorder via headphones. The preparation of the tape which includes all the test items requires care. Many studies have used synthetic speech for the verbal material, as any differences between the left and right ear stimuli can be tightly controlled. These synthetic stimuli can be generated and presented by computer.

Whatever stimuli are chosen, the right ear set and the left ear set are generally recorded separately on two different mono reel-to-reel tape recorders assuming the tape method is adopted. The individual tokens are then edited out of the master tapes onto tape-loops, and the outputs of the two mono tape recorders are coupled up to a dual beam storage oscilloscope. The recorders are put into playback mode, and the intensity of the two signals is adjusted with the help of the gauges on the recorders to be the same. Then, by gradually moving the tape loops, the onset of the two tokens can be made simultaneous as shown by the traces on the oscilloscope. Normally such a procedure will guarantee simultaneous onset of the token pair to within ± 2 msec. Once the simultaneity of onset and equivalence of signal amplitude has been achieved, the token pair can be recorded directly from the mono machines onto the two channels of a stereo tape recorder, where one channel is linked to the left ear of stereo headphones, the other to the right.

Apart from the creation of the dichotic tape, various factors must be considered in the design of the experimental procedure. Firstly, the nature of the tokens must be decided. Often linguistic and non-linguistic tokens are included, the latter being represented by music, tones or everyday 'environmental' noises. More frequently, however, studies have concentrated solely on linguistic stimuli, choosing whole words, syllables, or digits. One of the preferred methods utilizes sets, of CVC (consonant–vowel–consonant) words, such as 'gap-cap', 'cap-cab', or nonsense syllables, such as 'pa', 'ba', 'ta', 'da', 'ka', 'ga'. As can be seen from these examples, the phonetic difference between the pair is usually confined to a single segment difference to keep the discrimination task as straightforward as possible.

The next decision must be the mode of presentation and response. Some studies have presented groups of stimuli before requiring a response, e.g. three pairs of stimuli and then three responses and so on. The disadvantage here is that this relies on an efficient auditory retention ability, which may well be affected in certain clinical populations. Therefore, it may well be advisable to require a response following each presentation.

The order of presentation must also be organized to ensure a quasi-random distribution of stimulus types. Random in that no set order must be obvious, but organized in such a way that repeated and transposed pairs are evenly distributed throughout the presentation. Stimuli are normally repeated two or three times to rule out external effects, and test pairs are normally transposed, so that 'cap-gap' will also appear as 'gap-cap' to ensure that it is the dichotic effect that is responsible for the results, not any inherent perceptual characteristics of the sounds involved (i.e. phonetic effects).

Finally the method of response must be settled. Studies have utilized various methods. 'Forced-choice' involves the subject in making a single choice for each presentation, whereas 'free-recall' allows the subject to report as many items as possible from whichever ear. 'Precued partial report' requires the subject to report what is thought to be the left ear or right ear as indicated by the tester. Whichever method is chosen, various modes are found: oral report, written report, or gestural where the subject points to the correct form from an array of usually two or four possible answers.

Dichotic listening and normal subjects

The majority of right-handed normal subjects clearly demonstrate a right-ear preference (REP) for verbal material, and a left-ear preference (LEP) for non-verbal material. By this we mean that on dichotic listening tests using words, the right ear forms are 'heard' more often than their left-ear pairs, and vice versa with non-verbal pairs. This effect has helped us to look at how the brain processes sound: both linguistic and non-linguistic. As shown in Figure 31.1, there are two auditory pathways from each inner ear to the cortex: the contralateral pathway which leads from the right ear to the left hemisphere of the brain and vice versa, and the ipsilateral pathway which leads to the same side hemisphere as the ear. The contralateral pathway is the stronger and more efficient of the two and inhibits the signal

Figure 31.1 The contralateral and ipsilateral auditory pathways

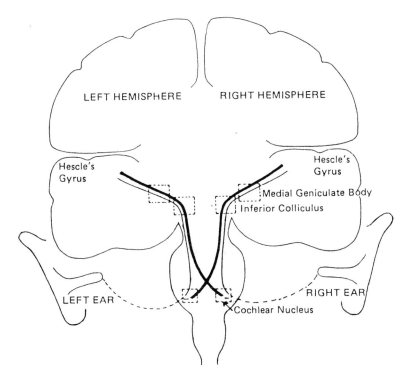

of the weaker ipsilateral pathway. Using this information we can account for REP in verbal stimuli by the fact that it appears to be the left hemisphere that has superiority in verbal processing, so the signal from the right ear will appear stronger. The roles are reversed for non-verbal material, where it seems the right hemisphere has superiority in processing. Of course, dichotic listening measures ear preference directly, from which we *infer* hemispheric specialization.

Researchers have used the technique with normal populations, then, to examine if there are any correlations between degrees of hemispheric specialization (as shown indirectly by the test) and factors such as handedness (left or right), age, and sex. In terms of the age variable it would appear that hemispheric specialization may well not be present at birth but develop later, perhaps at puberty, and may continue to change and develop throughout life.

Sex differences in hemispheric specialization have also been investigated, and it appears that there may well be a lesser degree of lateralization in women than in men, and women seem to demonstrate a more bilateral representation of language.

With handedness, the left-handed section of the population (amounting to some 10 per cent) seem to divide into two groups under dichotic listening conditions. About half of the left-handed subjects studied show REP for verbal stimuli just as right-handed subjects. The other half show bilateral or right-hemisphere specialization for linguistic stimuli.

Certain reservations have been made about the reliability of the procedure. It is known that there are in-built perceptual preferences for some sounds over others, so care must be taken to ensure a phonetically balanced set of tokens, otherwise the results may be distorted. Further, concern has been expressed at the low test–retest reliability of dichotic listening: in one study nearly a third of the subjects (all normals) changed their ear preferences on retest.

Dichotic listening and language disordered subjects

The two groups of patients with which dichotic listening studies have been used most are aphasics and stutterers. With both these groups researchers have been trying to discover whether the normal pattern of left-hemisphere specialization for language has been disturbed. If this is the case, it not only tells us something about the nature of the disorder itself, but may well aid in the planning of remediation through, with aphasics for example, the bolstering of the role of the *right* hemisphere in taking over language function.

The difficulty in interpreting results from dichotic tests with aphasics is the separation of the lesion effect from the dominance effect. The lesion effect is the impairment to a greater or lesser extent of stimuli presented to the ear contralateral to the lesion, while the dominance effect is the normal right- or left-ear hemisphere dominance dependent upon the material presented. Despite this problem, several studies have come to the conclusion that these effects can be separated. This is because there are consistent results from these studies suggesting that LEP increases in many types of aphasia over time since onset of the disorder. This has been interpreted as a change in dominance patterns, as the lesion effect would not be expected to alter over time.

Stutterers are the other major group of language disordered who have been studied with dichotic listening. We can summarize the findings of many of these studies here. It would appear that separate sub-groups of stutterers exist, some of which have ear-preferences similar to non-stutterers. Others, however, seem to lack this lateralization and have bilateral representation of language. Some researchers believe this may explain why certain child stutterers may spontaneously become fluent. They speculate that this is due to a later than usual development of hemispheric specialization, thus removing the 'cause' of the disfluency. As with aphasic studies, further research is needed on stuttering and hemispheric specialization, and it may be that techniques other than dichotic listening will be needed.

Conclusion

Dichotic listening gives us a fascinating glimpse into the workings of the brain in the interpretation of speech. However, it is known that the pathways between the ears and the brain, and between the two hemispheres are still only partly understood, and so the interpretation of dichotic results is still open to considerable uncertainty.

Further reading

Code and Ball (1984) again provides further reading on this technique and its application in the clinic. For readers who wish to explore further the implication of this research for our understanding of the brain and language, and of aphasia, Code (1987) is recommended, but this is not an introductory level text.

CHAPTER 32

Time-Variated Speech

In Chapter 30 we examined the importance of the temporal aspect of feedback in speech, but there is another time-related aspect to speech production and perception: that of tempo or speech rate. It is clear that the rate of utterances has a part to play in their comprehension, and that an excessively fast or slow tempo will be likely to produce a measurable effect.

In recent times researchers have begun to investigate what happens to both normal and disordered speakers when listening to time-variated speech. From this it may be that comparison between the responses of normal and disordered subjects may serve as a diagnostic measure and tell us more about the speech perception process.

In this chapter we will discuss the various methods of temporally altering the speech signal, and the results of comprehension studies with both normal and disordered populations.

Techniques of time-variated speech

The simplest method of changing the normal speech rate of a verbal stimulus is the 'non-instrumental' approach. This requires only that the testers alter their own speech rate, either up or down, and that this is then used in the investigation. There are, however, several drawbacks to this method. Firstly, there are limits to the extent that humans can alter their speech rates, e.g. the maximum increase will be about 30 per cent. Further, it will be difficult to maintain a particular increase with any precision beyond just a few words. Also, such non-instrumental changes are likely to distort the normal temporal relations between individual segments or parts of segments in an uncontrolled way.

Another simple approach involves 'playback variation' of tape-recorded speech samples. The original message is played to subjects at either a faster or slower speed than the recording. The disadvantage here is also distortion, in that the change in speed brings about changes in the frequency. This means that tests using this method will be examining subjects' responses to frequency distortion as well as time variation.

The approach which seems to be the most successful in this field is termed 'sampling', and there are three different sampling techniques: manual, electro-mechanical, and electronic. Generally speaking, all sampling procedures involve a segmentation of the speech signal, with some portions discarded and some retained in order to cut down on distortion. They differ in the means employed to segment the signal.

With manual sampling the researcher literally segments the tape by cutting out sections of the tape, and then splicing the remaining portions together again, perhaps with the addition of small sections of silence. If done well, this can produce quite an acceptable end result, but if care is not taken, a jerky and distorted speech signal can still be the outcome. To be practicable the original signal must be recorded at a very fast speed, and the necessary work is tedious and can take a great deal of time.

To get round these difficulties, an electromechanical approach was developed using a 'time compressor–expander' invented in the 1950s. This utilizes a tape-loop and a special type of tape recorder. During playback of the tape-loop (which contains the relevant speech portion) the machine automatically omits parts of the signal and joins the remainder together in one new signal. Naturally, this will produce a 'quicker' rate, but the machine can produce a 'slower' speech rate by automatically inserting into the signal short repeated segments. While it is possible to choose how many samples the machine should discard or repeat, it is not possible to choose which particular parts of the signal should constitute these samples. Also, the equipment necessary for electromechanical sampling is costly, and too large to be convenient.

More recently, a purely electronic instrumentation has been developed for varying speech tempo. While working in principle in a way similar to the electro-mechanical approach, electronic sampling involves the use of mini- or micro-computers. It is thus more controllable in terms of what aspects of the signal are to be altered, and is more convenient in terms of size and price.

As with delayed auditory feedback and dichotic listening, test procedures with time-variated speech require a response from the subjects, either verbally or gestur-ally. In this case what we are measuring is the intelligibility of the speech signal under time variation. However, as with the other procedures described in the previous two chapters, care must be taken in devising the stimuli. Stimuli that are linguistically 'too easy' (containing, perhaps, too many linguistic cues as to the meaning) will be unlikely to produce interesting results. Likewise, if the alteration to the signal is only slight, changes in the ability to understand the stimulus will not be great.

Time-variated speech and normal subjects

There have been many investigations of the response of normal subjects to the alter-ation of speech rate (mostly in terms of speeding up the stimulus). Some of the early studies have been criticized on methodological grounds, but work in the 1970s has given us a good idea as to patterns of intelligibility in these circumstances.

A study of a large group of young adults is described here. The subjects had to listen to four lists of monosyllabic words at six different rates of compression (0, 30, 40, 50, 60 and 70 per cent), and at four different intensity levels: 8, 16, 24 and 32 dB. The results of this study are shown in Figure 32.1.

Figure 32.1 The effects of time variated speech: mean percentage correct scores for normal hearing young adult listeners on the four NU-6 monosyllabic word lists, under time compression conditions of 0% and 30–70% in 10% steps; each list and compression condition presented at 8, 16, 24, and 32 dB

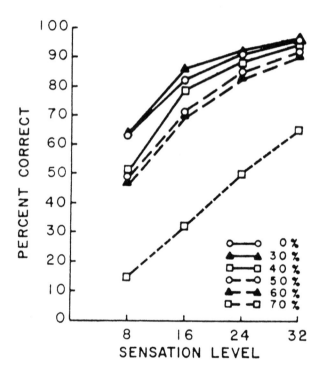

It can be seen, as expected, that intelligibility in all conditions increased in parallel with the increase in intensity. Also, intelligibility decreases as the per-centage of compression increases. This change is most marked between 60 and 70 per cent compression. Other studies have confirmed that 70 per cent compression in sampling methods appears to be an important cut-off point, though if the play-back variation system is used, then 30 per cent compression creates this major loss of intelligibility. Studies with older subjects confirm the general trend of Figure 32.1, but show a major drop in intelligibility occurring at a lower level of time compression (about 40 per cent). With children there is an interaction between age and amount of compression, as well as to some extent the linguistic nature of the stimulus. Generally speaking, the responses improve with age, but the point of major loss of intelligibility remains, as with the young adults, at about 60 per cent compression.

There have been many 'follow-up' studies on time-variated speech, to see if it is possible to isolate which features of the speech signal add to or detract from intelligibility under this non-normal condition. Amongst the features studied in this respect are grammaticality, length of the test utterance, and differences between word lists, full sentences and so on. It would appear from some of these studies that length of stimulus has little effect, but time-expanded stimuli are easier than compressed ones, and that grammatically complex sentences are easier than simple ones. It has also been shown that apparently similar word lists can produce startlingly different results, as can different speakers of the stimuli.

Time-variated speech and disordered subjects

The main clinical population that have been used in time-variated speech research has been the aphasic group. As with dichotic listening, experiments with this group have been designed to investigate differences of response between the two ears. Not only can this be used diagnostically in an attempt to aid the classification of the aphasia type, but will aid research into the role of the various neural pathways in perception and comprehension.

An example of the use of the procedure in diagnostics can be seen in the case of a patient where non-time compression techniques suggested that there was brain-stem involvement in the disorder. Time-compressed stimuli were also used as part of the assessment, and these suggested that impairment was also present in the temporal lobe, and this subsequently proved to be the case.

Other groups of adult speech-disordered patients have also been tested with time-variated speech. These include patients suffering from various kinds of peripheral (i.e. non-central) hearing loss, and stutterers. Studies on sensorineural deaf subjects show a regular drop in scores compared with normals, and in particular that a 40 per cent compression rate produces marked lowering in intelligibility.

Researchers have also used time-variated speech in studies of childhood speech disorders, particularly problems of articulation. Such studies show these children behave similarly to normals at 0 and 30 per cent rate of compression, but are significantly worse at 60 per cent.

An interesting development related to the study of misarticulation is the use of time-expanded procedures. Here, speech samples from misarticulating children (or indeed adult aphasics, and other groups) are expanded and used in the training of speech pathologists and clinical phoneticians. Such procedures have produced interesting results. Using three rates, 0, 150 and 200 per cent expansion, groups of student clinicians showed marked improvement in recognition at the expanded rates.

There have been numerous other studies using time-variated speech with clinical populations, and we do not have the space to go into these here. One particularly interesting area for further research is whether slowed speech can be used to help aphasic patients understand speech, and indeed have their own speech understood. To this end we would need, as in DAF, to see the development of small portable time-variated speech machines.

Conclusion

Time-variated speech, like the other two auditory techniques described in this part of the book, has shown its worth in both diagnosis and research. However, time-variated speech unlike DAF and dichotic listening perhaps, encompasses such a range of effects that there is still some way to go before we understand fully what it can tell us about the normal process of perception and comprehension, and about disturbances to these normal patterns.

Further reading

The authoritative introduction to time-variated speech research, and the source of the various studies described in this chapter is Riensche, Orchik and Beasley (1984), which in turn provides further references in the area for interested readers.

APPENDICES
Phonetic Symbols and Notes on Transcription

APPENDIX 1

THE INTERNATIONAL PHONETIC ALPHABET (Revised to 1979)

	Bilabial	Labiodental	Dental, Alveolar, or Post-alveolar	Retroflex	Palato-alveolar	Palatal	Velar	Uvular	Labial-Palatal	Labial-Velar	Pharyngeal	Glottal
Nasal	m	ɱ	n	ɳ		ɲ	ŋ	ɴ				
Plosive	p b		t d	ʈ ɖ		c ɟ	k g	q ɢ		k͡p g͡b		ʔ
(Median) Fricative	ɸ β	f v	θ ð s z	ʂ ʐ	ʃ ʒ	ç ʝ	x ɣ	χ ʁ			ħ ʕ	h ɦ
(Median) Approximant		ʋ	ɹ	ɻ		j	ɰ		ɥ	w		
Lateral Fricative			ɬ ɮ									
Lateral (Approximant)			l	ɭ		ʎ						
Trill			r					ʀ				
Tap or Flap			ɾ	ɽ				ʀ				
Ejective	p'		t'				k'					
Implosive	ɓ		ɗ				ɠ					
(Median) Click	ʘ		ʇ									
Lateral Click			ʖ									

(pulmonic air-stream mechanism) — S, T, N, V, N, O, S — *(non-pulmonic air-stream)* — N, O, C

VOWELS

	Front	Back	Front	Back
Close	i • ɨ	ɯ u	y ʉ	u
Half-close	e ə	ɤ o	ø •	o
Half-open	ɛ	ʌ ɔ	œ	ɔ
Open	æ ɐ	a ɑ	œ	ɒ
	Unrounded		Rounded	

OTHER SYMBOLS

- ɕ, ʑ Alveolo-palatal fricatives
- ʃ, ʒ Palatalized ʃ, ʒ
- ɭ Alveolar fricative trill
- ɺ Alveolar lateral flap
- ɧ Simultaneous ʃ and x
- ɿ Variety of ʃ resembling s, etc.
- ɪ = ι
- ʊ = ω
- ɜ = Variety of ə
- ɚ = r-coloured ə

DIACRITICS

- ˳ Voiceless n̥ d̥
- ˬ Voiced s̬ t̬
- ʰ Aspirated tʰ
- ˷ Breathy-voiced b̤ a̤
- ˌ Dental t̪
- ˌ Labialized t̫
- ʲ Palatalized t̫
- ˞ Velarized or Pharyngealized t̴, ɫ
- ˌ Syllabic n̩ l̩
- ̯ or ˌ Simultaneous ʃ (but see also under the heading Affricates)
- · or ̇ Raised e·, ẹ, e̝ w
- · or ̣ Lowered e·, ẹ, e̞ ɵ
- ̣ or ˌ Advanced u·, u̟
- ˌ or ̠ Retracted i·, i̠, t̠
- ̈ Centralized ë
- ̃ Nasalized ã
- ˎ, ʵ r-coloured a˞
- ː Long aː
- · Half-long a·
- ̆ Non-syllabic ŭ
- ˑ More rounded ɔ̹
- ˏ Less rounded y̜

STRESS, TONE (PITCH)

ˈ stress, placed at beginning of stressed syllable: ˌ secondary stress: ˉ high level pitch, high tone: ˏ low level: ˊ high rising: ˎ low rising: ˋ high falling: ˴ low falling: ˇ rise-fall: ˆ fall-rise.

AFFRICATES can be written as digraphs, as ligatures, or with slur marks: thus ts, tʃ, dʒ: t͡s t͡ʃ d͡ʒ: c, ɟ may occasionally be used for tʃ, dʒ.

APPENDIX 2

PRDS Symbols (Recommended Phonetic Symbols for the Representation of Segmental Aspects of Disordered Speech)

A. *Relating mainly to place of articulation*

1. Bilabial trills   ppp b͡bb
2. Lingualabials   plosives, nasal   P B M
   (tongue tip/blade   fricatives   ꝑ 8
   to upper lip)   lateral   L
3. Labiodental plosives and nasal   p̪ b̪ m̪
   (m̪ is an alternative to the usual ɱ)
4. Reverse labiodentals   plosives, nasal   p̺ b̺ m̺
   (lower teeth to   fricatives   f̺ v̺
   upper lip)
5. Interdentals   plosives, nasal   t̪̟ d̪̟ n̪̟ (or t̟ etc.)
   (using existing IPA
   convention for advancement)
6. Bidentals   fricatives   h̪ ɦ̪ (or ꝫ etc.)
   (lower teeth to   percussive
   upper teeth)
7. Voiced palatal fricative   ʝ
   (reserving j for palatal approximant)
8. Voiced velar lateral   ʎ̠
   (using existing IPA
   convention for retraction)
9. Pharyngeal plosives   q̠ ɢ̠
   (using existing IPA
   convention for retraction)

B. *Relating mainly to manner of articulation*

10. Segments with nasal escape:
    (i) nasal fricatives (audible   m̥ᶠ mᶠ n̥ᶠ ŋᶠ etc.
    turbulent nasal egressive
    air-flow; no oral escape)
    (ii) nasalized fricatives   s̃ z̃ x̃ etc.; also s̃ᶠ etc.
    (iii) sounds intermediate between   t̃ d̃ p̃ etc.
    oral stop and nasal

NOTE: The nasality diacritic, [˜], may be freely used to denote nasal resonance or escape; it does not in itself imply nasal *friction*, for which the raised [ᶠ] is recommended.

11. Lateral fricatives with sibilance   ɬ̬ ꞵ etc.; or ɬ̬ʃ etc.
12. Strong/tense articulation   } *   f̬ m̬
13. Weak/lax/tentative articulation }   f̰ m̰
   *as compared with the norm for
   the segment in question
14. Reiterated articulation   p͡p͡p etc.
   (as in dysfluencies and palilalia)
15. Alveolar slit fricatives   θ̱ ð̱
   (using existing IPA
   convention for retraction)
16. Blade (as opposed to tip of tongue)   s̻ t̻
   articulation
17. Plosive with non-audible release   p̚ b̚

C. *Relating to vocal fold activity*
18. Unaspirated   p$^=$ t$^=$ etc.
   (where explicit symbolization is
   desired)
19. Pre-voiced; post-voiced   ˌz z˳ etc.
   (i.e. with voicing starting earlier/
   continuing later than the norm for
   the segment in question)
20. Partially voiced (for segments   ˌs s˳ etc.
   normally voiceless; use where 's̬'
   etc. is not sufficiently explicit)
21. Partially voiceless (for segments   ˌz z˳
   normally voiced; use where 'z̥' etc.
   is not sufficiently explicit)
22. Preaspirated   ʰp ʰt etc.

D. *Relating to air-stream mechanism*
23. Pulmonic ingressive   s̩ m̩ etc.
24. Oral (velaric) egressive   ǀ̩ etc.
   ('reverse click')
25. Zero air-stream (absence of air-stream   (f) (m) etc.
   mechanism, but articulation present;
   'silent articulations', 'mouthing')
   NOTE: This may occur simultaneously
   with an articulation using some other
   air-stream mechanism, e.g.   ʔ(f) ŋ(f)

E. *Relating to duration, coarticulation, and pausing*
26. Excessively short   m̆ θ̆ ʒ̆ etc.
   NOTE: It is felt that confusion is unlikely to arise between this use and the customary IPA use
   to denote non-syllabicity; but this diacritic should *not* be used to denote mere absence of
   length.
27. Prolonged   m: (or m::) etc.
   (using existing IPA conventions)   p: (i.e. with prolonged
              hold/closure stage)

28. Silence, with absence of coarticulatory
    effects between segments or words
    short   –   thus ʌn–dɔ
    long   – –   ʌn – – dɔ
    extra long   – – –   ʌn – – – dɔ

F. Relating to secondary articulation
29. Lip rounding (using existing IPA   s̫
    convention for labialization)
30. Lip spreading   s̩

G. Relating to inadequacy of data or transcriptional confidence
31. 'Not sure'   Ring doubtful symbols
                                                  or cover symbols, thus:

    ◯   entirely unspecified articulatory segment

    Ⓒ   unspecified consonant

    Ⓥ   unspecified vowel

    Ⓢ   unspecified stop

    Ⓕ   unspecified fricative

    Ⓐ   unspecified approximant

    (NAS)   unspecified nasal

    (AFF)   unspecified affricate

    (LAT)   unspecified lateral

    (PAL)   probably palatal, unspecified manner (etc)

    ⓘ   probably [ɨ], but not sure (etc.)

    mɪ(ɤ)(k) probably [ɤk], but not sure (etc.)

    Note: A voiced, but otherwise unspecified, fricative may be shown as Ⓕ ; similarly, a
    voiceless, but otherwise unspecified, stop as Ⓢ ; and so on.
32. Speech sound(s) masked by   (( ))
    extraneous noise   thus   bɪg ((bæd wʊl))f
                                              or   bɪg ((2 sylls))
33. *The asterisk.* It is recommended that free use be made of asterisks (indexed, if necessary)
    and footnotes where it is desired to record some segment or feature for which no symbol is
    provided.

Reproduced by kind permission of the King Edward's Hospital Fund for London.

Notes on Phonetic Transcription

This book is not intended as a guide to phonetic transcription so we cannot go into this topic in any great detail. Nevertheless, we have spent some considerable space in introducing the phonetic symbols necessary to transcribe normal and aspects of disordered speech, and consequently I have decided to include a few notes of guidance in their use.

To undertake good phonetic transcriptions it is, of course, necessary that you have had a competent phonetics teacher who was able to pronounce the different sounds in relation to the symbols; you cannot learn the sound of a phonetic symbol from a book! It is not sufficient just to learn the symbols that correspond to the sounds of English: in speech pathology a whole range of non-English sounds may occur, not to mention features from other accents of English, or speakers of other languages you may come into contact with.

In ideal circumstances students should avail themselves of taped material with which to practice and improve their skills at recognizing speech sounds. Video tapes can also be very important here, as often visual cues can be vital in distinguishing certain sounds that differ little in their acoustic make-up: for example bilabial and labiodental consonants.

When it comes to making an actual transcription it is important that the transcriber divorces him/herself as much as possible from their linguistic background. In other words attempt to limit the effect that your knowledge of the language has on what you expect the subject to say. Chapter 25 outlined the marked effect that linguistic expectations can have on what we think we hear, so try avoiding this by doing practice transcriptions on taped examples of a language you do not know. Then you must attempt to take that frame of mind with you when you undertake clinical work. This last point is of particular importance for speech pathologists and clinical linguists, in that we need as accurate a record of the patient's speech as possible, not simply the nearest phonemic equivalent. Without an accurate description we are unable to provide a meaningful diagnosis, or prepare a helpful remediation plan.

If the transcription forms part of a piece of research, you should always consider the possibility of providing some sort of validation of your accuracy by having another phonetically trained person transcribe the material, or at least a representative portion of the material. The two transcriptions can then be compared for inter-transcriber agreement. In this sort of procedure one normally looks to agreement rates of 90 per cent or better. In the case of disagreements, the participants will check to make sure that they are not simply due to disagreements as to what a symbol stands for, or what symbol to use for a particular sound (e.g. [š] or [ʃ]. In other instances, repeated listening to the tapes may settle disagreements, but it is likely that a few will still remain. Remaining disagreements are not important as long as they are only a small percentage, but should there be a large number of these that cannot be settled, a third transcriber may have to be called in to settle the problem.

The actual mechanics of understanding transcriptions can cause problems in that the process is time-consuming and so can become boring. While it is important to undertake the task as soon as possible after the session so that any cues you picked up there remain fresh in your mind, it may be that the tape-listening sessions should be broken up into sections of no more than half an hour to avoid your attention wandering. To some extent the time-consuming continual rewinding of the tape machine can be improved through the use of machines with review and cue switches which allow you to move the tape back and forward without switching the play button off. If you can video-tape the session as well, that will allow you to back up the audio stimulus with a visual record.

Although recent computer packages are making it possible to produce phonetic symbols mechanically, for most speech pathologists the resultant phonetic transcription will be presented in hand-written form. It is important, then, that this is clear and unambiguous. It should be stated whether the transcription is intended to be read as phonemic or phonetic, though this can, of course, also be shown by the use of the appropriate brackets (slants for phonemic, square for phonetic). Any diacritics used should be clear, as it is easy to confuse some of them. The symbols themselves should be kept separate from each other, as cursive forms (i.e. joined-up versions) can also cause confusion. Take care that symbols that 'sit' on the line are not confused with those that have ascenders or descenders, as in the example of secondary cardinal vowel [ʊ] as compared to the voiced velar fricative [ɣ]. Finally, if you need to use symbols for disordered speech, make sure you note which systems you are utilizing, as there is as yet no international agreement in this field.

It is hoped that these few notes will guide you to the production of transcriptions of patients' speech that will actually aid in diagnosis and remediation, rather than just stay unexamined in the file.

References

ABBERTON, E. and FOURCIN, A. (1984) Electrolaryngography, in Code, C. and Ball, M.J. (eds.), *Experimental Clinical Phonetics*, Beckenham, Croom Helm.

ABBERTON, E., HOWARD, D. and FOURCIN, A. (1989) Laryngographic Assessment of Normal Voice – a tutorial. *Clinical Linguistics and Phonetics*, 3, 281–96.

ABERCROMBIE, D. (1965) *Studies in Phonetics and Linguistics*, London, Oxford University Press.

ABERCROMBIE, D. (1967) *Elements of General Phonetics*, Edinburgh, Edinburgh University Press.

ANTHONY, J. and HEWLETT, N. (1984) Aerometry, in Code, C. and Ball, M.J. (eds.), *Experimental Clinical Phonetics*, Beckenham, Croom Helm.

ARONSON, A. E. (1980) *Clinical Voice Disorders*, New York, Thieme Stratton.

BALL, M.J. (1984) X-ray techniques, in Code, C. and Ball, M.J. (eds.), *Experimental Clinical Phonetics*, Beckenham, Croom Helm.

BALL, M.J. (1988a) The contribution of speech pathology to the development of phonetic description, in Ball, M.J. (Ed.), *Theoretical Linguistics and Disordered Language*, Beckenham, Croom Helm.

BALL, M.J. (1988b) A diacritic range for phonation types. *Journal of the International Phonetic Association*, 18, pp. 39–40.

BALLANTYNE, J. (1977) *Deafness*, 3rd ed., London, Churchill Livingstone.

BEAGLEY, H. (Ed.) (1981) *Audiology and Audiological Medicine*, Oxford, Oxford University Press.

BLADON, R. and NOLAN, F. (1977) A videofluorographic investigation of tip and blade alveolars in English. *Journal of Phonetics*, 5, pp. 185–93.

BORDEN, G. and HARRIS, K. (1980) *Speech Science Primer*, Baltimore, Williams and Wilkins.

BROSNAHAN, L.F. and MALMBERG, B. (1970) *Introduction to Phonetics*, Cambridge, Cambridge University Press.

CANEPARI, L. (1983) *Phonetic Notation/La Notazione Fonetica*, Venice, Cafoscarina.

CATFORD, J.C. (1977) *Fundamental Problems in Phonetics*, Edinburgh, Edinburgh University Press.

CATFORD, J.C. (1988) *A Practical Introduction to Phonetics*, Oxford, Oxford University Press.

CODE, C. (1987) *Language, Aphasia and the Right Hemisphere*, Chichester, John Wiley.

CODE, C. and BALL, M.J. (1982) Fricative production in Broca's aphasia: a spectrographic analysis. *Journal of Phonetics*, 10, pp. 325–31.

CODE, C. and BALL, M.J. (Eds.) (1984) *Experimental Clinical Phonetics*, Beckenham, Croom Helm.

CODE, C. and BALL, M. J. (1988) Apraxia of speech: the case for a cognitive phonetics, in Ball, M. J. (Ed.), *Theoretical Linguistics and Disordered Language*, Beckenham, Croom Helm.

CRYSTAL, D. (1980) *Introduction to Language Pathology*, London, Edward Arnold.

CRYSTAL, D. (1982) *Profiling Linguistic Disability*, London, Edward Arnold.

DALTON, P. and HARDCASTLE, W. (1977) *Disorders of Fluency*, London, Edward Arnold.

DELATTRE, P., LIBERMAN, A., COOPER, F. and GERSTMAN, L. (1976) An experimental study of the acoustic determinants of vowel color, in Fry, D. (Ed.), *Acoustic Phonetics*, Cambridge, Cambridge University Press.

DENES, P. and PINSON, E. (1973) *The Speech Chain*, New York, Anchor Books.

DEW, D. and JENSEN, P. (1977) *Phonetic Processing: The Dynamics of Speech*, Columbus, Ohio, Charles E. Merrill.

EDELS, Y. (Ed.) (1983) *Laryngectomy. Diagnosis to Rehabilitation*, Beckenham, Croom Helm.

FANT, G. (1973) *Speech Sounds and Features*, Cambridge, Mass., MIT Press.

FARMER, A. (1984) Spectrography, in Code, C. and Ball, M. J. (Eds.), *Experimental Clinical Phonetics*, Beckenham, Croom Helm.

FAWCUS, M. (Ed.) (1986) *Voice Disorders and their Management*, Beckenham, Croom Helm.

FRY, D. (Ed.) (1976) *Acoustic Phonetics*, Cambridge, Cambridge University Press.

FRY, D. (1979) *The Physics of Speech*, Cambridge, Cambridge University Press.

FUJIMURA, O. (1962) Analysis of nasal consonants, *Journal of the Acoustical Society of America*, **34**, pp. 1865–75.

GREENE, M. (1973) *The Voice and its Disorders*, 2nd ed., London, Pitman.

GRUNWELL, P. (1987) *Clinical Phonology*, 2nd ed., Beckenham, Croom Helm.

HALLIDAY, M. A. K. (1970) *A Course in Spoken English: Intonation*, London, Oxford University Press.

HARDCASTLE, W. JONES, W., KNIGHT, C., TRUDGEON, A. and CALDER, G. (1989) New developments in electropalatography: A State-of-the-art report. *Clinical Linguistics and Phonetics*, **3**, 1–38.

HOLDSWORTH, W. (1970) *Cleft Lip and Palate*, London, Heinemann.

HUGHES, G. and HALLE, M. (1956) Spectral properties of fricative consonants. *Journal of the Acoustical Society of America*, **28**, pp. 303–10.

IPA (1979) *Principles of the International Phonetic Association*, London, IPA.

JASSEM, W. (1962) The acoustics of consonants, in Sovijärvi and Aalto, P. (Eds.), *Proceedings of the 4th International Congress of Phonetic Sciences*, The Hague, Mouton. (Also in Fry, 1976).

JOHNS-LEWIS, C. (1986) *Intonation in Discourse*, Beckenham, Croom Helm.

JONES, D. (1922) *Outline of English Phonetics*, 2nd ed., Leipzig, B. G. Teubner Verlag.

JONES, G. E. (1984) The distinctive vowels and consonants of Welsh, in Ball, M. J. and Jones, G. E. (Eds.) *Welsh Phonology: Selected Readings*, Cardiff, University of Wales Press.

KATZ, J. (Ed.) (1985) *Handbook of Clinical Audiology*, Baltimore, Williams and Wilkins.

KELLER, K. (1971) *Instrumental Articulatory Phonetics: An Introduction to Techniques and Results*, Norman, Oklahoma, Summer Institute of Linguistics.

KOENIG, W., DUNN, H. and LACY, L. (1946) The sound spectrograph. *Journal of the Acoustical Society of America*, **17**, pp. 19–49.

KOHLER, K. (1984) Phonetic explanation in phonology: the feature fortis/lenis. *Phonetica*, **41**, pp. 150–74.

LADEFOGED, P. (1962) *Elements of Acoustic Phonetics*, Chicago, Chicago University Press.

LADEFOGED, P. (1967) *Three Areas of Experimental Phonetics*, London, Oxford University Press.

LADEFOGED, P. (1975) *A Course in Phonetics*, New York, Harcourt Brace Jovanovich.

LASS, R. (1984) *Phonology*, Cambridge, Cambridge University Press.

LAVER, J. (1980) *The Phonetic Description of Voice Quality*, Cambridge, Cambridge University Press.

LEHISTE, I. (Ed.) (1967) *Readings in Acoustic Phonetics*, Cambridge, Mass., MIT Press.

LEHISTE, I. (1970) *Suprasegmentals*, Cambridge, Mass., MIT Press.

LEHISTE, I. and PETERSON, G. (1961) Transitions, glides, and diphthongs. *Journal of the Acoustical Society of America*, 33, pp. 268–77.

LIBERMAN, A. M., DELATTRE, P. C., COOPER, F. S., and GERSTMAN, L. J. (1976) The role of consonant-vowel transitions in the perception of the stop and nasal consonants, in Fry D. (Ed.), *Acoustic Phonetics*, Cambridge, Cambridge University Press.

LUCHSINGER, R. and ARNOLD, G. (1965) *Voice-Speech-Language*, London, Constable.

MALMBERG, B. (Ed.) (1968) *Manual of Phonetics*, Amsterdam, North Holland.

MARTIN, F. (1981) *Introduction to Audiology*, Englewood Cliffs, NJ, Prentice Hall.

MARTIN, M. (Ed.) (1987) *Speech Audiometry*, London, Taylor and Francis.

MEADOW, K. (1980) *Deafness and Child Development*, London, Edward Arnold.

MILLER, N. (1986) *Dyspraxia and its Management*, Beckenham, Croom Helm.

MOORE, G. (1971) *Organic Voice Disorders*, Englewood Cliffs, NJ, Prentice Hall.

MOORE, W. (1984) 'Electromyography', in Code, C. and Ball, M. J. (Eds.) *Experimental Clinical Phonetics*, Beckenham, Croom Helm.

MORLEY, M. (1970) *Cleft Palate and Speech*, 7th ed., London, Churchill Livingstone.

NETSELL, R. (1973) Speech physiology, in Minifie, F., Hixon, T. and Williams, F. (Eds.), *Normal Aspects of Speech, Hearing, and Language*, Englewood Cliffs, NJ, Prentice Hall.

NETSELL, R. (1986) A Neurobiologic View of Speech Production and the Dysarthrias, San Diego, College Hill.

O'CONNOR, J. D. (1973) *Phonetics*, Harmondsworth, Penguin.

O'CONNOR, J. D. and ARNOLD, G. (1973) *The Intonation of Colloquial English*, London, Longmans.

ÖHMAN, S. (1966) Coarticulation in CVC utterances: spectrographic measures. *Journal of the Acoustical Society of America*, 39, pp. 151–68.

ÖHMAN, S. (1967) A numerical model of coarticulation. *Journal of the Acoustical Society of America*, 41, pp. 310–20.

PERKINS, W. H. and KENT, R. D. (1986) *Textbook of Functional Anatomy of Speech, Language and Hearing*, London, Taylor and Francis.

PETERSON, G. and BARNEY, H. (1952) Control methods used in a study of the vowels. *Journal of the Acoustical Society of America*, 24, pp. 175–84.

PETERSON, G. and LEHISTE, I. (1960) Duration of syllable nuclei in English. *Journal of the Acoustical Society of America*, 32, pp. 693–703.

PRDS GROUP (1983) *The Phonetic Representation of Disordered Speech*, London, The King's Fund.

PULLUM, G. and LADUSAW, W. (1987) *Phonetic Symbol Guide*, Chicago, University of Chicago Press.

RICHARDS, A. (1976) *Basic Experimentation in Psychoacoustics*, Baltimore, University Park Press.

RIENSCHE, L., ORCHIK, D. and BEASLEY, D. (1984) Time-variated speech, in Code, C. and Ball, M. J. (Eds.), *Experimental Clinical Phonetics*, Beckenham, Croom Helm.

ROSS, R. and JOHNSTON, M. (1972) *Cleft Lip and Palate*, Baltimore, Williams and Wilkins.

SHRIBERG, L. and KENT, R. D. (1982) *Clinical Phonetics*, New York, Macmillan.

SPRIGG, R. K. (1978) Phonation types: a reappraisal. *Journal of the International Phonetic Association*, 8, pp. 2–17.

STEMPLE, J. C. (1984) *Clinical Voice Pathology*, Columbus, Ohio, Charles E. Merrill.

STETSON, R. (1951) *Motor Phonetics*, 2nd ed., Amsterdam, North Holland.

STREVENS, P. (1960) Spectra of fricative noise in human speech. *Language and Speech*, **3**, pp. 32–49.

TATHAM, M. A. A. (1984) Recording and displaying speech, in Code, C. and Ball, M. J. (Eds.), *Experimental Clinical Phonetics*, Beckenham, Croom Helm.

TRAGER, G. and SMITH, H. (1957) *Outline of English Structure*, (revised ed.), Norman, Oklahoma, Battenburg Press.

TRUDGILL, P. (1986) *Dialects in Contact*, Oxford, Basil Blackwell.

WELLS, J. and COLSON, G. (1971) *Practical Phonetics*, London, Pitman.

WOLFF, J. (1973) *Language, Brain and Hearing*, London, Methuen.

WOOD, S. (1982) X-rays and model studies of vowel articulation. *Lund University Department of Linguistics Working Papers*, **23**.

Index